ABORT! RETRY! FAIL!

Second Edition

by Susan Klopfer

Revised by Faithe Wempen

alpha books

A Division of Prentice Hall Computer Publishing

11711 North College Avenue, Carmel, Indiana 46032 USA

©**1993 by Alpha Books**

SECOND EDITION
FIRST PRINTING—1993

International Standard Book Number: 1-56761-136-2
Library of Congress Catalog Card Number: 92-83857

96 95 94 93   8 7 6 5 4 3 2

Interpretation of the printing code: the rightmost number of the first series of numbers is the year of the book's printing; the rightmost number of the second series of numbers is the number of the book's printing. For example, a printing code of 93-2 shows that the second printing of the book occurred in 1993.

Printed in the United States of America

Marie Butler-Knight
Publisher

Lisa A. Bucki
Associate Publisher

Elizabeth Keaffaber
Managing Editor

Stephen R. Poland
Acquisitions Manager

Seta Frantz
Development Editor

Annalise N. Di Paolo
Production Editor

Audra Gable
Copy Editor

Bill Hendrickson
Cover and Interior Design

Steve Vanderbosch
Illustrator

Jeanne Clark, Tim Cox, Mark Enochs, Tim Groeling, Phil Kitchel,
Tom Loveman, Carrie Roth, Barbara Webster, Kelli Widdifield
Production Team

Special thanks to Kelly Oliver for ensuring the technical accuracy of this book.

Susan: For my parents, John and Betty; my husband, Fred; and my child, Barry.

Faithe: To my dad the Macintosh user, who will never know the joys of DOS error messages.

Susan Klopfer is a writer and trainer who has spent years teaching people how to use computers. She grew up in Oregon and Nevada and currently lives in Indianapolis.

Faithe Wempen is a development editor for Alpha Books. She is a Purdue University graduate and a computer enthusiast, and is the author of several Alpha Books titles, including the *One Minute Reference: DOS 6.*

Steve Vanderbosch is a staff artist for the *Indianapolis Star* and News. He has illustrated many of Alpha's best-selling titles, including *The Most PC for Your Money.*

Contents

INTRODUCTION

Why in the world would anyone title a computer book *Abort! Retry! Fail!*? If you're asking this question, you're probably a new PC user who's just learning about *DOS*, your computer's *Disk Operating System*.

DOS (rhymes with "floss") is very important to you and your PC. DOS is a language that allows various pieces of hardware (such as your PC and your printer) to talk to each other. DOS also acts as "interpreter" between the PC and the application software you run, such as your word processor or spreadsheet.

DOS is a wonderful invention, but it has a rather discourteous manner of communicating with human beings. The DOS messages that appear on your screen when something goes wrong are often quite impolite. They use words like "bad," "illegal," "incorrect," "error," and "invalid." These words can be pretty scary, especially if you don't know why your computer is giving you such a hard time.

Fortunately, this book can help.

How This Book Works

We've included in this book only the common messages and prompts that most PC users run into. Therefore, this is a smaller, friendlier book than the thick DOS manual that came with your PC.

Abort! Retry! Fail! is organized alphabetically by error message, warning, or prompt. For each listing you'll see

- the actual words that appear on your screen.
- what these words mean, in plain English.
- examples, or little stories.
- how to fix the problem.

Words that you see on-screen, or type on your keyboard, appear in a computer font, like this:

```
This is computer font.
```

You'll also see Tech tips along the way. These boxed notes provide extra information that's helpful—but not strictly necessary—to understanding the error message.

Many Versions of DOS

Sometimes you'll hear people talk about different brands of DOS, like MS-DOS or PC-DOS. In this book, we'll just call it DOS. There are differences between them, but none worth bothering with.

You will also hear people talk about version numbers. That's because every now and then DOS is improved. (After all, the programmers who write this stuff need to buy new cars, too.) Each time DOS is changed, there's a new version number. Right now, there are six major versions of DOS, with several minor versions.

In this book we'll focus on version 6.0, with some of the common version 5.0, version 4.01, and version 3.3 messages cross-referenced.

Some software packages (such as a word processor) produce their own sets of DOS-like messages and prompts, like Not a valid filename. The message is usually similar enough to a DOS error message that you can figure out what it means. Also, the manual that came with the software often has its own listing of error messages.

Acknowledgments

Thanks to Susan Klopfer, the author of the first edition, for much of the wit and humor contained herein, and to Steve Poland, Acquisitions Manager, for allowing me to revise the book for DOS 6.0.

Thanks also to the many people at Alpha Books who made the manuscript into a book: Seta Frantz, Development Editor; Annalise Di Paolo, Production Editor; and Audra Gable, Copy Editor. Special thanks to Kelly Oliver for ensuring the technical accuracy.

And to the first edition's crew, whose good work made our job easier this time around: Barry Childs-Helton, Joe Kraynak, Liz Keaffaber, Lisa Bucki, Ed Guilford, and Herb Feltner.

Thanks also to those hard-working folks in the production department at Prentice Hall Computer Publishing.

Trademarks

information. Use of a term in this book should not be regarded as affecting the validity of any trademark or service mark.

CP BACKUP is a trademark of Central Point Software.

DOS 3.3, 4.1, 5.0, and 6.0 are trademarks of Microsoft Corporation.

MS BACKUP is a trademark of Microsoft Corporation.

MS-DOS is a registered trademark of Microsoft Corporation.

Norton Disk Doctor is a trademark of Symantec Corporation.

PKLITE and PKZIP are trademarks of PKWare Inc.

STACKER is a registered trademark of Stac Electronics.

A filename with that first character already exists. Press any key and then re-type the first character.

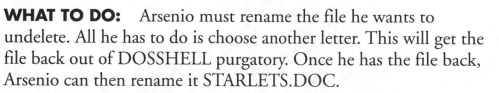

DESCRIPTION: DOS gives you a second chance if you delete a file accidentally. Here, you're in DOS 5.0 or 6.0 using DOSSHELL and try to undelete a file using the first letter of the deleted file to recover it. The letter you enter creates a file name that already exists in the specified directory.

EXAMPLE: Arsenio is recovering a file and needs to fill in a letter to retrieve ?TARS.DOC. He types S but gets a message that another STARS.DOC file already exists. So he types P and the file reappears.

WHAT TO DO: Arsenio must rename the file he wants to undelete. All he has to do is choose another letter. This will get the file back out of DOSSHELL purgatory. Once he has the file back, Arsenio can then rename it STARLETS.DOC.

Abort, Retry, Ignore, Fail?

DESCRIPTION: Whenever you see an error message on your screen, followed by Abort, Retry, Ignore, Fail (or a shortened version), this says a device error has occurred.

3

DOS harrumphs this classic message—sometimes leaving out the options to Ignore or to Fail—when it's waiting for you to jump in and *do* something, like close a drive door or turn on the printer.

DOS may have tried to read or write to a drive, printer, or some other device. Things didn't work out, so DOS tells you to get cracking and fix the problem. With Abort, Retry, Ignore, Fail, you'll always get another message. Here are some examples:

```
Data error reading drive...

File allocation table bad...

General failure writing drive...

Not ready reading drive...

Read fault error reading drive...

Sector not found

Sharing violation

Write protect error writing drive...
```

EXAMPLE: For a closer look at any of these examples, look up the specific messages (such as *Sector not found*) in this book.

If you're working within a software application, such as a word processor, and you forget to turn on the printer or close the drive door (or if there is a similar device error), you'll most likely get a less terse message that is similar to a DOS error message, along with some combination of Abort, Retry, Ignore, and Fail.

a

WHAT TO DO: DOS is patient. Your computer will wait. . . and wait. . . until you fix the problem, if you can. If you can figure out what the problem is (like leaving a diskette out of the drive or not closing the drive door), fix it and press **R** for Retry. DOS will try again to do what it's supposed to do, and the error may never return.

If you can't figure out why you're getting this error message—and the message keeps popping up on the screen every time you press **R**—then press **F** for Fail, or **A** for Abort. DOS will usually allow for a graceful exit.

a

Abort and Fail are not the same options; they work a little differently. Abort will actually end the application (program) that is making the request for device read or write. Fail will terminate the specific operation DOS is performing—but the application will continue. As a rule of thumb, try Fail before trying Abort. (Fail is not available in DOS versions before 3.3. Darn!)

Let's say you're trying to access a floppy drive that has no disk in it. If you choose F—out of desperation and a desire to go home someday to your spouse and family—you'll get a message like this:

```
Current drive is no longer valid>
```

Just type in **c:** and press **Enter**, and you'll return to the C: drive. Here's how this would look:

```
Not ready reading drive B
Abort, Retry, Fail?f
Current drive is no longer valid>C:
C:\>
```

If Ignore is an option, and you choose it, DOS will just pretend that nothing happened. That is, the computer will try to skip the error it found (such as a bad sector) and continue with your command. However, this may result in data loss, so it's not recommended.

If all else fails, reboot by pressing **Ctrl-Alt-Del**. This is a last-ditch response because it will cause you to lose all unsaved work.

Access Denied

DESCRIPTION: You'll get this message if

- You tried to delete a file marked Read-Only.

- You tried to open a subdirectory as a file (in DOS versions other than 3.x).

EXAMPLE: At Joan's company, various levels of security are assigned to critical accounting files. Some accountants can access and make changes to these files—while other employees, like Joan, are given a "read only" status. When Joan attempts to delete an accounting file, she gets the message Access Denied.

WHAT TO DO: You can remove the file's read-only attribute using the ATTRIB command. Doing so changes this particular *attribute* of a file from read-only to read/write. It's best for Joan, however, to discuss the problem with her supervisor before she attempts to change the status of the file. It was set up this way for a reason.

All files in directory will be deleted!
Are you sure (Y/N)?

a

DESCRIPTION: You'll get this warning message when you try to delete all of the files in a directory or subdirectory. (For DOS 3.x, only Are you sure (Y/N)? appears.)

This message appears for your own safety. It allows you the option of choosing whether to complete the Delete command. Answering Y to this question will erase all the files.

EXAMPLE: Computer nerds like to nuke files; it's fun to give a wild-card command telling DOS to erase all of the files in a subdirectory—to whisper, "Fire one!" and then choose Y. Try it on a Friday afternoon. Copy a bunch of files into a subdirectory named JUNK. If you want to try deleting just the copied files with a .TXT extension, type in

```
C:\JUNK>del *.txt
```

and press **Enter**. To delete *all* the JUNK text files, type in

```
C:\JUNK>del *.*
```

and press **Enter**.

The *.* uses *wild-card characters* and says to erase every file in the JUNK subdirectory—regardless of the file name and regardless of the extension. You'll get the question

```
All files in directory will be deleted!

Are you sure (Y/N)?
```

Respond with **Y** or **N**. Answering Y will delete all your text files. Then you can check out the power of this command by typing in

```
C:\JUNK>DIR
```

and pressing **Enter**. You'll see that the deleted files are all gone!

WHAT TO DO: Just be certain that you *really do want* to delete all the files in a directory before you press that Y key.

Allocation error, size adjusted

DESCRIPTION: This message erupts during CHKDSK, along with the name of a specific file. It means that the size of this file doesn't match the space allocated for it in the File Allocation Table (FAT).

EXAMPLE: Walt frequently runs the DOS command CHKDSK (Check Disk) to check up on his PC. He wants to know things like what shape his files are in, how much storage capacity is on his disk, how many bad sectors there are, and how much RAM is available for running programs. This time Walt gets the `Allocation error`, `size adjusted` message, and he sees that the filename LETTER.DOC, one of his Microsoft Word files, is listed.

WHAT TO DO: If a corrupted data file has no backup file to restore from, type **CHKDSK /F** to fix the FAT. This will change the file's size as listed in the directory entry; however, you might lose some of the information stored in the file.

Since Walt's file is a document, it's in his best interests to restore as much of the file as he can. So he uses CHKDSK /F and recovers all but the last two lines of the letter. If Walt's file had been a program file (such as WORD.EXE), he would have had to restore it by first deleting the file from his drive and then restoring the file from the copy he made of his original word processing software disk.

Follow Walt's lead. As a safe computing practice, always make copies of your original software disks and use these copies for installation and restoring files.

ANSI.SYS must be installed to perform requested function

DESCRIPTION: You'll get this message if you need to install a special device driver called ANSI.SYS. ANSI.SYS makes it possible to show "graphics" when your monitor is operating in text mode. Older shareware games often require this.

EXAMPLE: Tom gets some great shareware educational software. But when he tries to run it on his PC, Tom gets the ANSI.SYS must be installed message because his PC hasn't loaded ANSI.SYS into memory.

ANSI.SYS is one of DOS's own device drivers that uses standards set by the American National Standards Institute (hence, ANSI). According to the ANSI standards, this file defines functions, or operations, that control your PC's display graphics, cursor location, and key reassignments.

WHAT TO DO: Make sure your CONFIG.SYS file holds a DEVICE= command that lists ANSI.SYS. It might look like this:

```
DEVICE=C:\DOS\ANSI.SYS
```

or like this, if your PC can access upper-memory blocks:

```
DEVICEHIGH=C:\DOS\ANSI.SYS
```

After you've put this line into your CONFIG.SYS file, you must reboot your computer to load the driver into memory.

Are you sure (Y/N)?

See *All files in directory will be deleted!*

A20 hardware error

a

DESCRIPTION: This message appears as your computer is starting up. The DOS=HIGH line in your CONFIG.SYS triggers this message if your computer hardware does not allow the A20 address to be used. This sounds complicated, but it isn't really. It just means that a quirk in your particular model of computer is preventing DOS from loading itself into high memory.

You'll only get this message if you're using DOS 5.0 or DOS 6.0, because earlier versions didn't support DOS=HIGH.

EXAMPLE: Denise has a 286-based computer made by a manufacturer that no one has ever heard of. She has endured the taunts of her friends for years, knowing that her system cost less than a quarter of what they paid.

When Denise bought DOS 5.0, the back of the box promised her that she would be able to load DOS into high memory and free up some of her conventional memory. She carefully followed the instructions in the manual—she added the line DOS=HIGH to her CONFIG.SYS file, then held her breath in anticipation while she rebooted. Instead of a great memory savings, however, she got the message A20 hardware error. She was relieved that her friends weren't there to see it.

WHAT TO DO: You can always buy a new computer if you're in the same fix as Denise. But that's a drastic measure. A less expensive option is to take the DOS=HIGH line out of your CONFIG.SYS file. (It's not necessary; it's just an improvement that frees up some memory.)

DOS 5.0 has lots of fancy new features, most of which work with any computer. However, way back in the mid-eighties, many manufacturers "did it their way," and there was a lot of nonstandard hardware produced. By the late eighties, manufacturers had pretty much decided on a standard, and today everything works about the same from vendor to vendor.

If you have one of these nonstandard machines, it will work fine for most purposes, so don't despair. Just get used to the fact that not every nifty trick that DOS can do is going to work on your machine.

a

Bad command or file name

DESCRIPTION: You made a mistake when you were typing in a DOS command, and DOS didn't know what you wanted it to do. You may have misspelled a name, left out a needed disk drive or path name, or left out the command altogether and just typed in a file name. It's also possible that the file you are trying to access may not exist—or may be in a directory that DOS does not see at the moment.

EXAMPLE: Jerry wants to copy the file SCR.TXT from the WORD subdirectory in the C: drive over to the A: drive, but he forgot to type in the word *copy*. The result would be

```
C:\WORD>scr.txt a:

Bad command or file name
```

See what happens when the COPY command is left out? Here's another example where misspelling the command's name brings up the error message:

```
C:\WORD>cpy scr.txt a:

Bad command or file name
```

WHAT TO DO: Make sure you type in commands carefully and correctly. If you get this message, look for possible spelling errors or check to see if you left out the command entirely.

If you're sure you've typed correctly, the problem may be DOS's inability to find the program. Make sure the program you are trying to run actually exists and that DOS can find it.

DOS "finds" a program if the program is in the active directory (such as C:\WORD in the example above), or if the PATH statement includes the directory. (The PATH statement is usually set in the AUTOEXEC.BAT file.) When you type in a command, DOS looks first in the active directory, and then in each of the directories in the PATH statement, until it finds the program. If the program is not in any of those places, you get the `Bad command or file name` *error message. You can find more information about altering the search path in the DOS manual.*

b

Bad or missing Command Interpreter
Enter correct name of Command Interpreter
(eg. C:\COMMAND.COM)

DESCRIPTION: Now you've really done it! DOS can't find its boss! How would you feel if your company president suddenly left town? DOS depends solely on its command interpreter (COMMAND.COM) to act as an interpreter between you and the computer. If it can't find COMMAND.COM, DOS will simply curl up and refuse to speak.

The second line of the message is unique to DOS 6.0; you won't see it with earlier versions.

EXAMPLE: Wanda was experimenting with the SYS command and made a bootable floppy disk from a diskette in her A: drive. Then, during the course of her day, she needed a disk to hold some data, so she deleted all the files from A: (DEL A:*.*) and filled up the diskette with data files.

Now, a diskette needs 3 files to be bootable. Two of them, MSDOS.SYS and IO.SYS, are hidden, so when Wanda typed DEL A:*.* they didn't get deleted. But the other one, COMMAND.COM, was wiped out.

The next time Wanda turns on her computer, she forgets that the disk is still in the A: drive. DOS tries to load itself from A:, since it finds 2 of the 3 files it needs there but can't finish because it needs COMMAND.COM.

Wanda chuckles at her own carelessness, removes the diskette from A:, presses Ctrl-Alt-Del, and boots flawlessly from the hard drive.

WHAT TO DO: It depends on what is happening when you get the message.

Scenario #1: You are booting (starting up) your computer from a floppy disk.

If you're using DOS 6.0, you have the opportunity to enter a path to COMMAND.COM, as the second line of the error message prompts you to do. For example, if you are booting from A:, where there's no COMMAND.COM, you can direct DOS to the COMMAND.COM file on C: by typing `C:\COMMAND.COM`.

If you're using any other version of DOS, you need to reboot with a different floppy disk (the one that came with your computer is a good choice). This is why you keep your manuals and extra diskettes nearby.

Scenario #2: You are booting from your hard disk.

Your COMMAND.COM file has probably been deleted from your hard disk. To fix the problem, simply copy COMMAND.COM from your original DOS diskette to the root directory of your hard disk.

Scenario #3: You are exiting from an application program.

Perhaps you have accidentally deleted COMMAND.COM while in your application program. The first thing to try is this:

1. Reboot your computer using the original system disk that came with your computer or another bootable floppy disk.

2. Copy COMMAND.COM from the bootable disk to your root directory (`COPY A:COMMAND.COM C:\`).

3. Remove the floppy disk from the A: drive.

4. Press **Ctrl-Alt-Del** to reboot.

If that doesn't work, then perhaps the application can't locate COMMAND.COM when it exits, even though it's there. You can help DOS locate COMMAND.COM by setting a COMSPEC variable in your AUTOEXEC.BAT file. Here's how:

1. Restart your computer, but don't enter the application program that's causing the problem.

2. Using a text editor program such as EDIT, add the following line to your AUTOEXEC.BAT file:

```
SET COMSPEC=C:\COMMAND.COM
```

3. Save the file and restart your computer.

b

What's this COMSPEC variable all about? Well, some application programs dump a portion of COMMAND.COM out of memory to make more room for themselves. That's fine, but then COMMAND.COM must be reloaded when you exit the program.

If the program is on a drive different than COMMAND.COM is, DOS may get confused and not remember where COMMAND.COM is kept. The COMSPEC variable tells DOS to remember COMMAND.COM's location at all times.

Bad or missing *filename*

DESCRIPTION: This is a startup warning message and says that DOS is supposed to load a device driver that can't be located or that the device driver was loaded but something was wrong with it (or something else along those lines). DOS will keep booting, but won't use the device driver.

So what's a device driver and why does this matter? It is a program that allows the operating system to work with a specific piece of hardware, like a printer or a mouse. Device drivers are loaded from the CONFIG.SYS file in your root directory at startup. This tells DOS to use the particular driver.

EXAMPLE: During the boot (startup), Gina sees this message scroll by on the screen. She couldn't exactly read which file it referred to, since it went by so quickly. But then when she tried to run a program that she normally used her mouse with, the mouse didn't work!

Gina investigated by displaying her CONFIG.SYS file on the screen. (She used the command `TYPE CONFIG.SYS` from the root directory.) Sure enough, the line for the mouse driver had a typo in it. It read

```
DEVICE=C:\moose.sys /Y
```

when it really needed to say

```
DEVICE=C:\mouse.sys /Y
```

She used a text editor (like EDIT) to change the line back to MOUSE, rebooted, and all was well again.

Some mouse drivers are loaded with MOUSE.COM files rather than MOUSE.SYS, and reside in AUTOEXEC.BAT. So if you're looking for the mouse driver line in CONFIG.SYS and don't find it, peek in AUTOEXEC.BAT. However, it won't say "DEVICE=" *there—it'll just say MOUSE (or MOOSE!) or maybe C:\MOUSE.COM.*

b

WHAT TO DO: If DOS can't load a device driver, several things could be wrong:

- The line in the CONFIG.SYS or AUTOEXEC.BAT that calls the driver could be misspelled or could show the driver (mistakenly) in a directory other than the one it actually occupies.

- The device driver file could have been deleted, moved, or damaged.

- A file compression program you are using (such as PKLITE) could be incompatible with that particular driver.

If the CONFIG.SYS or AUTOEXEC.BAT is wrong, change them using a text editing program such as EDLIN or EDIT. Piece of cake! Then go find the nasty rat who played around with your CONFIG.SYS file in the first place!

If the device driver has been moved, deleted, or damaged, copy it back to where it's supposed to be—from an original diskette. If file compression is the culprit, decompress the file, or delete it and recopy from the original diskettes. (Hint: the command for decompressing with PKLITE is PKLITE *filename.ext* -x.)

b

Bad partition table

DESCRIPTION: If you want to, you can divide your hard disk into different "logical" disks, each part with its own drive letter. This is called *partitioning*. (The real, "physical" drive never actually separates.) You set this up with the FDISK command. Then, when you actually FORMAT the logical disk, DOS creates a partition table to store information that tells your PC how many partitions the disk has and where the operating system's Startup files are.

You'll see this Bad partition table message if you're trying to format one of these logical disks and DOS can't find the right partition information.

EXAMPLE: Alice's PC has a very large hard disk. She wants to take advantage of this fact and create separate partitions so she can run another operating system (like UNIX) on one of them. DOS won't even have to know that a competitor is lurking in the recesses of the PC.

First, Alice makes a complete backup of her existing hard disk. Then she uses a special command called FDISK to divide her hard disk into a primary partition (which holds DOS and is bootable) and a secondary partition (which can be divided up into even more logical drives with names like D:, E:, or even Z:). She'll move her UNIX operating system into D:.

About 40 minutes into this project, Alice is formatting drive D:, and DOS gives her a `Bad partition table` messsage. How strange! DOS can't find the correct partition information for Alice's disk.

WHAT TO DO: Alice can try the rerun FORMAT, but she probably will need to run the FDISK program again to create new (or correct) DOS partitions on her hard disk. Then she can try again to format the newly created logical drives, including drive D: for UNIX.

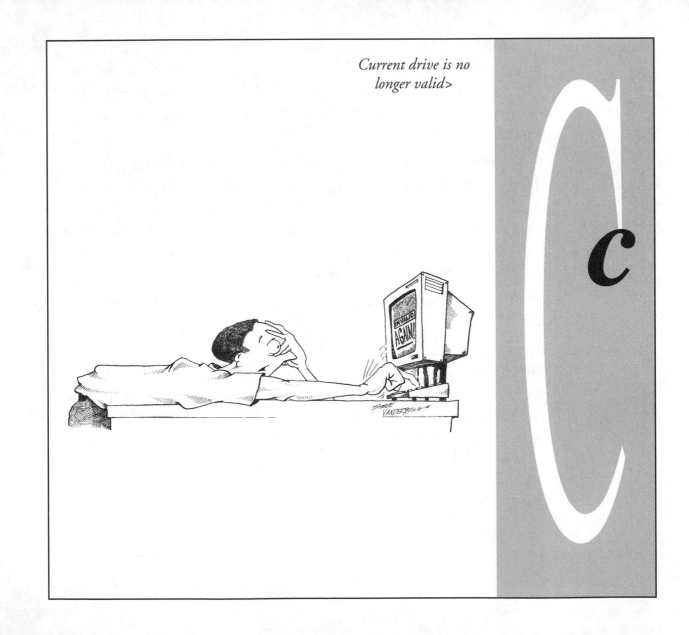

Cannot diskcopy hard disk media

See *Specified drive does not exist or is non-removable.*

Cannot execute *x*

See *Error in exe file.*

Cannot load COMMAND, system halted

See *Invalid COMMAND.COM, system halted.*

C

Cannot Loadhigh batch file

DESCRIPTION: You have a 386 or 486 machine and DOS 5.0 or 6.0 (call me psychic!). You've tried to load a batch file into high memory, and you've just learned that it can't be done.

EXAMPLE: Terri has been studying her DOS manual all afternoon, and has learned how to load device drivers and TSRs (terminate-and-stay-resident programs) into high memory. She has already saved over 30K of conventional memory, and is still going strong. (Okay, so Terri's a bit of a computer geek!)

Having finished adding DEVICEHIGH= lines to her CONFIG.SYS file, Terri turns to her AUTOEXEC.BAT file and adds LOADHIGH= to the beginning of each line so the programs will "load high." Then she reboots and sees `Cannot Loadhigh batch file` scrolling up her screen.

WHAT TO DO: LOADHIGH= is a wonderful thing. It can move mouse drivers and other memory-resident programs out of your "workspace" (conventional memory) and into otherwise-wasted high memory. However, it can only do this with certain kinds of programs, and batch files (files that end in .BAT) are not one of them.

You don't have to fix this problem if you don't mind seeing the error message each time you boot. When DOS cannot load a program high, it loads it normally, so you're still okay. But if you want to stop the error message, edit your AUTOEXEC.BAT file and remove the LOADHIGH= from the beginning of any lines that have .BAT in them.

Cannot make directory entry

DESCRIPTION: You might see this message if you try to create a file or directory in the root directory of a disk that already contains lots of files and/or directories. The message is telling you that the file allocation table (FAT) for the disk can't keep track of any more items.

EXAMPLE: Hank likes to keep his hard disk nice and neat. His job requires him to work with lots of little graphics files; and whenever he gets 100 or so of them accumulated, he copies them onto floppy disks for storage.

One day when Hank has accumulated about 150 files in a directory called GRAPHICS, he pops a 360K floppy disk into his A: drive and types

```
COPY C:\GRAPHICS\*.* A:
```

Hank has already checked the size of the graphics files, and he knows that all 150 of them only add up to 300K, so he assumes they will all fit on one disk. But after the 112th one, DOS tells him Cannot make directory entry.

WHAT TO DO: A disk's File Allocation Table (FAT) keeps track of the root directory contents, both files and subdirectories. Each file and each subdirectory takes up a slot in the table. When the table is full, that's it! No more items allowed!

The exact number of items allowed depends on the disk type. For example, a high density 3.5" disk can hold 224 items, while a high density 5.25" disk can hold only 112.

In Hank's case, he could have created a subdirectory on the diskette and copied his files into it. Since subdirectories are not

C

limited in the amount of files they can hold, all 150 would have fit easily!

Of course, if Hank goes to create a subdirectory on his disk now, DOS won't let him because all the slots are still taken. He'd have to delete one of his graphics files from the diskette first.

Cannot setup expanded memory

DESCRIPTION: You're seeing this message because you were trying to use FASTOPEN with the /x switch, but you don't have any expanded memory available.

FASTOPEN is a DOS command that speeds up opening files and directories by creating a name cache in memory that stores their disk locations.

EXAMPLE: Lou has just installed an expanded memory card, and wants to put it to use. He tries to use the /x switch to force FASTOPEN to place its cache in expanded memory.

However, when setting up the new card, Lou forgot to add a DEVICE= command for it in his CONFIG.SYS file. So Lou's plan misfires, and he gets this Cannot set up expanded memory message on his PC screen instead.

WHAT TO DO: Check your CONFIG.SYS file and see if it really has all of the required commands to load your expanded memory manager or emulator. This information is part of the documentation that accompanies your expanded memory board, and can also be found in your DOS manual.

Like Lou, you'll need special commands to set up extended memory, special commands to let DOS use the upper-memory blocks, and special commands to link upper-memory blocks with conventional memory.

If the CONFIG.SYS is set up correctly and it still doesn't work, your memory card may be bad.

C

Some people who don't have an expanded memory board use a device driver like DOS's EMM386.EXE to make their extended memory pretend to be expanded memory. If the line in CONFIG.SYS that activates this driver contains an error, it could trigger this error message.

Cannot start COMMAND, exiting

DESCRIPTION: You'll see this message if DOS is attempting to load an additional copy of COMMAND.COM. (You might be using a function key or command to call DOS from within a word processor.)

EXAMPLE: You are in Microsoft Word 5.5 with a "plain vanilla" system, 640K RAM. You use the DOS Command option to try to get the DOS prompt. The message `Cannot start COMMAND, exiting` appears.

WHAT TO DO: There are three possible causes of this problem. Most often, the error is caused by a FILES= statement in the CONFIG.SYS file. Therefore, the first course of action is to modify, or create, a FILES= statement in your CONFIG.SYS. Your current configuration may stipulate, for instance, `FILES=10`. You should increase this to **FILES=20** or **FILES=30**.

The second cause is related to memory—you don't have enough. If you're lucky, your computer's memory is being used by *terminate-and-stay-resident (TSR)* programs (such as SideKick) which can be removed. If this is the case, remove the TSRs from your AUTOEXEC.BAT file, and you might free up enough memory to avoid your problem. If this doesn't work, you may be able to add memory to your system.

Some older computers, called XTs, can't access memory greater than 640K. (They can sometimes use expanded memory boards, but expanded memory won't help in this situation.) So don't get taken to

the microchip cleaners—make sure your computer will support extra memory before you buy it.

Finally, it's possible there's an incorrect setting in your AUTOEXEC.BAT file. If the COMSPEC variable isn't set, or is set incorrectly, DOS won't be able to find COMMAND.COM. Look up *Bad or missing Command Interpreter* for details.

Convert lost chains to files (Y/N)?

DESCRIPTION: You'll get this message from a DOS program called CHKDSK (check disk). CHKDSK analyzes the disk's status, and can repair the map of where information is located on your disk.

If CHKDSK encounters pieces of old deleted files (or damaged files) that are not assigned space in the File Allocation Table (FAT), you'll get a message that says

```
xxx lost clusters found in yyy chains
Convert lost chains to files (Y/N)?
```

You can choose to save this lost information in separate files to look at later, or you can choose to delete it.

C

EXAMPLE: Jan is a heavy PC user—often creating, saving, and deleting some hefty files. In the past week, she's found that her PC seems to have electron deficiency anemia—tired circuits. She runs CHKDSK, hoping to perk the critter up.

She's greeted with the following message:

```
987 lost clusters were found in 15 chains

Convert lost chains to files (Y/N)?
```

This means there are a lot of pieces of lost files floating around.

Jan answers N to get back to the DOS prompt, then reruns CHKDSK with the /F switch: CHKDSK /F. When asked again about the lost clusters, Jan answers Y. DOS recovers each chain of lost information into a separate file whose name is in the form FILE*nnnn*.CHK, where *nnnn* is a number. Jan can then look at these files and see if the information is useful. If it isn't, she can delete the files.

If you run CHKDSK by typing CHKDSK *by itself, no matter which option you pick (Y or N), the problem will not be corrected. To correct the problem, you must use the /F switch with CHKDSK:* CHKDSK /F.

WHAT TO DO: If you are missing a data file (such as a letter or report), choosing Y is a good idea because you might be able to recover parts of it. Check out the .CHK files, and salvage what you can.

If you are missing a program file, just choose N; you'll never be able to patch the program back together in workable order.

Current drive is no longer valid>

DESCRIPTION: For some reason, DOS can't use the drive that is supposed to be current (active), so it's asking you to specify a different one.

Here's what you've been up to:

1. You tried to change to a drive that DOS couldn't read. (Maybe you typed A: when there was no disk in the A: drive.)

2. You then received some kind of error message (such as `General failure reading drive...`), followed by `Abort`, `Retry`, `Fail`? (or `Abort`, `Retry`, `Ignore` in DOS versions below 3.3).

3. And you chose F for Fail (or I for Ignore).

EXAMPLE: Tommy has been trying to access a disk in his A: drive, but has been getting the following error message:

C

```
General failure reading drive A

Abort, Retry, Fail?
```

Tommy isn't sure what the problem is, so he tries several times to select R for Retry. But the message just keeps coming back to haunt him. (If he looked closer, he would realize that he forgot to close the latch on the drive.) Daunted, he just wants to give up and move on, so he selects F for Fail. DOS reports

```
Current drive is no longer valid>
```

Tommy types a new drive letter, C:, and presses Enter, and he's back to his C: drive.

WHAT TO DO: Just type in a different drive letter (like C:) and press **Enter**; you'll change to the other drive.

C

Data error reading drive *x*
Abort, Retry, Fail?

DESCRIPTION: This message means that DOS can't read a file on your disk.

EXAMPLE: Joanie is having a busy day. She's been copying files back and forth from one disk to another.

Things are really rolling along, until Joanie, right in the middle of it all, gets a message that tells her DOS cannot read part of a file. No read? No write!

What is Joanie to do?

WHAT TO DO: If you're having the same problem as Joanie, you can first try pressing **R** for Retry. Go ahead and try this several times.

Sometimes DOS can read an "iffy" sector on the second or third try. If it doesn't work, choose **A** (Abort) to end the operation. Salvage individual files by copying them to a different disk; chances are only a small area of the disk is defective, and you will be able to save most of your files.

Don't use DISKCOPY in this situation; it probably won't work because of bad sectors.

After you've rescued all the files that you can from the disk, reformat it with the FORMAT command. If the problem returns, throw the disk away or return it to the manufacturer for a refund.

Directory already exists

DESCRIPTION: Maybe it's time for a break! You've tried to create a *new* directory or subdirectory, using a name that already exists in the current directory.

EXAMPLE: Margaret wants to reorganize her life. She's starting with her computer . . .

A friend told Margaret she can create special indexes (or *subdirectories*) to keep track of files by categories, using the MD command. For instance, she's going to set up subdirectories in her word processor for each of the projects she's working on.

When Margaret names a subdirectory *WP* (for Whitehall Project), she gets the `Directory already exists` message. The name of her current directory is also WP (for word processing).

WHAT TO DO: If you share Margaret's dilemma, you can first try to resolve the conflict by coming up with another name for a subdirectory.

In this case, Margaret can simply change the name of her subdirectory to WHP and she'll be fine.

d

Disk boot failure

DESCRIPTION: This message appears if something goes afoul when DOS tries to load itself into your PC's memory during startup.

There's a small amount of permanent memory in your PC, but the majority of the memory is Random Access Memory (RAM), which is erased each time the power goes off. Each time you start your PC, the operating system gets reloaded into RAM.

When you flip the switch, a program contained in that small permanent memory space kicks in and loads the needed operating system files—allowing your PC to get moving, or boot (a techie term for "pull itself up by its own bootstraps"). During booting, your PC gets tested and prepared to accept your keyboard commands. DOS lets the hardware and software communicate, and DOS controls how your PC will interact with the display, keyboard, and drives.

EXAMPLE: Zoe just came up with a great idea, and wants to do some hurry-up-before-I-forget-it word processing on her PC. She switches on the power, her PC makes a few grinding sounds, and then halts as `Disk boot failure` appears on her screen.

WHAT TO DO: Try correcting this problem by *soft booting* (pressing **Ctrl-Alt-Del** or the **RESET** button). If you soft boot several times and continue to get this message, try shutting off your PC for twenty seconds and then restarting your system.

If the problem still doesn't go away, try putting your original DOS diskette into drive A: and booting the computer from it. Then use the SYS command to transfer the system to your hard disk. (If your hard disk is C:, type `sys c:`.) Then copy COMMAND.COM from your A: drive to your hard disk.

It's always a good idea to have a *system diskette* handy. When you format diskettes using the format command by itself, you're preparing a *data* diskette. Data diskettes aren't system diskettes because they don't have the three crucial DOS files on them (COMMAND.COM plus two hidden system files, usually called IO.SYS and MSDOS.SYS).

To format a diskette as a *system* diskette, you add /s to your FORMAT command. For example, to format a system diskette using the A: drive, you would type `FORMAT a:/s` and then press **Enter**.

Disk error writing FAT x

DESCRIPTION: PCs are tidy, well-managed creatures. They systematically keep track of every file you feed them in a special record called the *File Allocation Table (FAT)*. (They even keep two identical copies, in case of problems!) But in spite of all this organization, things occasionally go wrong. This message appears when there are problems updating the FAT.

EXAMPLE: Adam is running CHKDSK, and he sees `Disk error writing FAT` x appear on his screen as the CHKDSK program tries to update the file allocation table (FAT). This means that a disk error was discovered during the process.

There are two copies of the FAT; the x indicates the particular copy that is causing the problem. For example, if the x appears as a number 1, the first copy of the file allocation table can't be written.

WHAT TO DO: There are two kinds of people in this world: people who've lost data, and people who *will* lose data. So, a wonderful rule to live your life by is: *always back up your files before you do a CHKDSK*. From this example, the reason why is pretty clear.

In this case, the File Allocation Table (FAT) that was specified has a bad sector and can't be used. Try to copy your files to another disk. Then try running a CHKDSK with the /F option on the original disk, and—just maybe—it will correct the error. If this doesn't work, try a commercial program such as the Norton Disk Doctor.

If the error still isn't corrected, your files are lost; you can try to FORMAT the disk to use it again. If it's a floppy and bad sectors are reported, *toss it.* If you're working with a hard disk and the FORMAT fails, you could have a serious problem, in which case you need to talk to a service representative.

Disk full. Edits lost.

DESCRIPTION: Any changes you make with EDLIN to a PC file are lost when you see this message. Your disk is full, and there isn't enough space to save your newly edited file.

EXAMPLE: Zack is editing a batch file with EDLIN. As he ends the session (by typing **e** or **end**) expecting his changes to be saved, he gets this message instead:

```
Disk full. Edits lost
```

*How about that EDLIN! If you haven't been introduced, EDLIN stands for **ED**it **LIN**e. It comes with every version of DOS except DOS 6.0. It's a seemingly simple editor that lets you edit one line at a time. (EDIT, a much better tool than EDLIN, can be substituted for EDLIN in DOS 5.0 and above, making life a whole lot easier.)*

WHAT TO DO: Get out a blank diskette (or find a spot on your fixed drive), copy your original file onto it, and start editing again. Sorry.

Disk full. Writes not completed

See *Disk full. Edits lost.*

Disk unsuitable for system disk

DESCRIPTION: This diskette was earmarked to be a system disk, but it's a little bit messed up and can only be used for data. You'll never be able to boot your PC from it.

EXAMPLE: Samantha has decided to make up a batch of fresh system diskettes to have on hand in case her PC should ever crash. She is formatting a diskette using the /S switch (for system), and during the process, DOS discovers a bad track where DOS files are supposed to reside. Her computer tells her

```
Disk unsuitable for system disk
```

WHAT TO DO: You'll need to find a different diskette to make your system diskette. The one you have here can only be used for data.

Divide overflow

DESCRIPTION: This is an error that shouldn't happen. You'll see it if you're running a defective program, or if the data in a file or a program has been messed up, forcing an illegal act to happen (such as dividing by zero).

EXAMPLE: Your neighbor has written a terrific piece of accounting software, and he wants you to test it for him. As you're running through some numbers, you suddenly get bounced out of the program, back into DOS—where the screen says `Divide overflow`.

WHAT TO DO: Bake some cookies. Eat them. Then go over to your neighbor's house and suggest that he do some debugging before you run his program again. If you *purchased* software that gives you this message, report the problem to the software dealer or publisher.

Drive not ready

This is the DOS Shell equivalent of *Not ready reading drive x.*

Drive not ready - cannot continue

See *Specified drive does not exist or is non-removable.*

Drive types or diskette types not compatible
Copy process ended
Copy another diskette (Y/N)?

DESCRIPTION: You're trying to copy a diskette using the DISKCOPY command. Either the disk in the source drive (for instance, drive A: in the command DISKCOPY A: B:) has a format different from that of the disk in the destination drive, or the disk is unformatted (or defective). The DOS 3.x version of this error message is Read error on source drive.

EXAMPLE: Jane wants to make an exact copy of her diskette which was formatted on her older PC in a 360K drive. She places the diskette in drive A: and she inserts a second diskette—which has a 1.44MB capacity—in drive B:. When she issues the DISKCOPY command, Jane gets this message.

WHAT TO DO: When you are copying diskettes using DISKCOPY, check the disks to be sure they're the same format. Both should be 360K, 1.2MB, or 1.44MB. If your disk drives are different, you will have to use the same drive for both source and destination (i.e. DISKCOPY A: A:).

45

Duplicate file name or file not found

DESCRIPTION: You wouldn't want your sister or brother to have your name, would you? You can't have two files with the same name, either. So, if you try to rename a file and use the same name for two files—or try to rename a file that doesn't exist (it happens!)—DOS is going to let you know.

EXAMPLE: Your neighbor is playing with your PC and destroys an important batch file titled SUSAN.BAT. You do have a backup of this file named SUSAN.BAK. You are going to rename SUSAN.BAK to SUSAN.BAT so you can use your backup, but you accidentally type REN SUSAN.BAK SUSAN.BAK. Since you typed the same name for both the source and the destination files, DOS will tell you the names are duplicates.

WHAT TO DO: This message is probably the result of a typo, so just type the command again. For example, you can bring the SUSAN file back into service—simply type an unused name for the destination, such as

```
ren susan.bak susan.bat
```

and you're back in business!

Execute failure

EMM386 not installed - other expanded memory manager detected

DESCRIPTION: You are trying to use DOS's EMM386 expanded memory manager, but you already have another expanded memory manager running. Since only one expanded memory manager can be active at a time, and the other one was there first, EMM386 refuses to load.

EXAMPLE: Tony has been using DOS 4.01 and Quarterdeck's QEMM for several years. QEMM has provided Tony with the memory management that he needed, and all in all he's been very happy.

When Tony upgrades to DOS 6, he decides to give DOS's equivalent of QEMM—EMM386.EXE—a try. He adds a line to his CONFIG.SYS file that installs EMM386. But QEMM is already there, in an earlier line of the CONFIG.SYS file. DOS tells him so with this error message.

WHAT TO DO: Tony can load any expanded memory manager he wants to, but he can only load one—QEMM or EMM386—not both.

If you're going to use a third-party memory manager such as QEMM, you don't need to mess with EMM386. Leave it out of your CONFIG.SYS file.

EMM386 not installed - XMS manager not present

DESCRIPTION: If you got this error message, you were booting your 386 or 486 computer with DOS 5.0 or 6.0 This message occurs when there is no HIMEM.SYS line before the EMM386.EXE line in your CONFIG.SYS file.

EXAMPLE: Marge has just installed DOS 6.0 and is trying to figure out how to load the expanded memory manager, EMM386.EXE. The DOS manual says to put a line in her CONFIG.SYS file like this:

```
DEVICE=C:\DOS\EMM386.EXE
```

But when she adds it, she gets this error message the next time she boots her computer! So she heads back to the DOS manual. In rereading the section on memory management, she learns that EMM386.EXE doesn't work by itself. It has to have an XMS manager loaded first, like HIMEM.SYS, before it will operate.

So Marge adds the following line right before the EMM386.EXE line:

```
DEVICE=C:\DOS\HIMEM.SYS
```

and when she reboots, she gets a message that EMM386 has been successfully installed!

WHAT TO DO: As Marge learned, EMM386.EXE doesn't work unless an XMS (extended memory) manager is loaded before it. DOS's extended memory manager is HIMEM.SYS, and it will do nicely for this purpose. (Some people prefer third-party managers like Quarterdeck's QEMM, but it's not necessary to buy a separate one unless you're a heavy-duty computer nut.)

If EMM386 isn't working, check your CONFIG.SYS file. You should see these two lines, in this order:

```
DEVICE=C:\DOS\HIMEM.SYS
DEVICE=C:\DOS\EMM386.EXE
```

Depending on many other factors, the wording might be a little different—"DOS" could be replaced by a different name, and the EMM386.EXE line might have "RAM" or "NOEMS" at the end. Other lines might be between these two, also. That's okay. Just make sure they're in this order.

Error in exe file

DESCRIPTION: You'll experience this message if DOS detects an error in an executable (.EXE) file while trying to run it. In DOS version 5.0, the error is worded Cannot execute *x*, where *x* is the program name.

This error could also occur if you're using a program designed for a different version of DOS. Ordinarily, when this happens, most programs will give you the `Incorrect DOS version` error message—but some poorly written programs will give you this one instead.

An .EXE extension on a file means that a program in this file is executable. You can run an executable file by keying in the file name at the prompt. For instance, if a program file is named TED.EXE, you can type in TED at the command line to activate the program.

EXAMPLE: Your cousin Jack has learned how to modify files with EDLIN and EDIT. Now he wants to give you a quick demo and brings up your WORD.EXE file in EDLIN. (Jack doesn't know that EDLIN is for *text* files, not *executables*.)

Jack doesn't practice safe computing. Instead of making a copy of your WORD.EXE file and placing it in a junk directory (or making certain there's already a backup file), Jack just plows ahead and makes changes. When Jack goes home, you try to start up your software and get this message.

WHAT TO DO: Here are some things to try if you get this error:

- If you're using purchased software, use your original disk to copy the .EXE files back into the appropriate directories. If the files are compressed, you may have to run the installation program again.

- If you're using new software for the first time, contact the dealer or publisher. The program is probably flawed.

- If you're using a self-written program, use LINK to produce another copy of the program. (If you know how to write programs, you probably understand how to use LINK. If not, see a DOS reference manual.)

e

Error in loading operating system

DESCRIPTION: If a disk error occurs while DOS is loading itself from the hard disk, and DOS can't boot, you'll see this message.

EXAMPLE: This just isn't your day. And to top it off, you try to boot your computer and get a message that says `Error in loading operating system`.

You call your cousin Jack for help, and he says to restart your computer. You do and your PC boots right up! Hmmm!

WHAT TO DO: Try to restart your computer before you panic. If the error occurs several times, try restarting DOS from your backup system diskette in a floppy drive and then changing to the C: prompt.

If DOS won't let you access the C: prompt, say you can't even bring up the directory, you'll have to contact your dealer because you probably have a hard disk problem.

If the hard disk *does* respond but isn't bootable, you'll need to reload the system files onto your hard drive. To do this, place your original DOS diskette in the floppy drive, log onto that drive, and type **SYS c:**. You might also need to copy COMMAND.COM to the hard disk. If the system cannot be transferred using the SYS command, it will be necessary to reformat the hard disk using the /S option.

e

Execute failure

DESCRIPTION: This message pops up if DOS runs into a problem while reading a command from disk, or if the FILES= command in the CONFIG.SYS file isn't set to a large enough value. If the problem is reading a command from disk, use the remedies explained in the entry for *Error in exe file*.

EXAMPLE: You just purchased a new game for your PC. You load it and give the command to let the game begin. Alas! No exploding missiles or raging dinosaurs appear on your PC—just a message that says Execute failure.

You remember that somewhere in the installation instructions there was something about altering a system file.

WHAT TO DO: You will probably need to use EDLIN or EDIT to increase the FILES= value in your CONFIG.SYS file. The documentation that came with the software should tell you what number to use. A common setting is 20.

CONFIG.SYS resides in the root directory of DOS and contains a list of special statements that define a nonstandard system configuration. It can be created and modified with a text editor like EDIT or EDLIN. Each line of the CONFIG.SYS file has the form command=value.

Increasing the FILES= value also decreases the available conventional memory; "more" is not always "better" where memory is concerned.

e

DESCRIPTION: DOS has a bouncer, Interrupt 24H—call him INT 24, for short. When you goof up, INT 24 usually receives an error code and then translates this code into a helpful message (like many of the ones in this book). If INT 24 doesn't get a code, you'll get the `Fail on INT 24` message.

EXAMPLE: Jon finds a 3 1/2-inch diskette in the bottom of his desk drawer and (quite naturally) wonders what is on it. He pops it into his B: drive and types

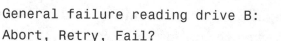

```
DIR B:
```

As it turns out, the disk isn't formatted, and he gets the message

```
General failure reading drive B:
Abort, Retry, Fail?
```

At this point, Jon realizes it's pointless to try to read this disk, but he's forgotten which option to choose. Surely not Retry, but is it Abort or Fail? He finally goes with Fail. (Bad choice, Jon. Abort is the easier way out.) DOS thinks Jon wants it to skip the part that it failed on and keep trying to read the disk. Of course, it fails again, and the `General failure` message comes back.

Jon, being rather feisty, tries F for Fail again when offered the `Abort, Retry, Fail?` choices, and DOS, having had enough of this unreadable disk, spits out `Fail on INT 24` and boots Jon back to the DOS prompt.

WHAT TO DO: If you received this message, then DOS should have terminated whatever it was doing and you should be back at the DOS prompt, ready to go. You can try what you were doing again, but chances are, you'll have to find another way to work around it. As for Jon, he'll have to format the disk before he can use it.

f

File allocation table bad, drive *x*
Abort, Retry, Fail?

DESCRIPTION: PCs keep systematic track of every file that is saved—in a special record called the *File Allocation Table (FAT)*. This message appears when DOS runs into a problem in the FAT of the disk in drive *x* (with *x* standing for the drive name, such as B:). You'll be given the option to Abort, Retry, Fail?. You might also be given the option to Ignore, depending upon the version of DOS you're using.

EXAMPLE: Pat is careless with her diskettes. She doesn't keep her diskettes in folders and she sometimes touches the exposed parts. She uses them for coasters when unexpected company arrives, and even smokes when she's using her PC.

One day, Pat tries to start up a program in drive B: using one of her ill-treated diskettes. The program bombs out and Pat gets the message File allocation table bad, drive b:.

Are we surprised?

WHAT TO DO: If you get this message, stay calm. Try entering **R** for Retry several times. If this does not solve the problem, use **A** for Abort. (See the entry for *Abort, Retry, Fail?*.) If you're using a diskette, attempt to copy all the files to another diskette and then reformat or junk the original diskette.

If you're using a hard drive, you may be able to back up all or some of the files on your drive and reformat. The drive is unusable until reformatted. A commercial program such as Norton Disk Doctor may be able to correct the problem with minimal data loss.

Meanwhile, take care of your diskettes:

- Don't leave diskettes in hot cars. Basically, keep your diskettes at room temperature.

- Store diskettes in their jackets, and in a diskette box or holder.

- Don't touch the exposed parts of the diskettes.

- Keep diskettes away from magnets, heat sources (such as the top of the monitor), strong electrical fields, and magnetized objects.

f

File cannot be copied onto itself

DESCRIPTION: It's okay—just a simple slip-up. You probably forgot to name a destination file while copying a file from one place to another. Or, you gave the same filename for both source and destination.

EXAMPLE: Claudius needs to copy an important fraternity file from his fixed drive to a floppy in his A: drive. He types

```
COPY club.doc
```

without including the destination, or a:, so DOS gives Claudius this message.

WHAT TO DO: Claudius just needs to add a: to his command, so that his instructions tell DOS where to send the copy. He types

```
COPY club.doc a:
```

and then everything is just fine.

File Creation Error

DESCRIPTION: This error occurs in certain instances if you attempt to add a new file name to the directory or to replace a file that was already there.

For example, try giving a file the same name as a volume, directory, or hidden (system) file and you'll get this message. `File creation error` also appears if the root directory is full—which will happen if you're holding 512 files and directories on a fixed drive, or even less on a floppy disk. This error also appears if the file you are naming already exists as a read-only file that can't be replaced.

EXAMPLE: Tommy wants to use EDLIN to build a batch file named COLLAGE.BAT. When he gives the command EDLIN COLLAGE, he forgets to attach .BAT. Because a subdirectory named COLLAGE already exists, he gets the message `File creation error`.

Tommy can still create a batch file under the name COLLAGE, as long as he adds .BAT as the extension.

WHAT TO DO: Look for other files with the same name you are attempting to use. If a file is there, check to see if it is marked "read-only" (using the ATTRIB command) and cannot be replaced. Is the file name the same as a subdirectory? Or the same as a system (hidden) file name?

You can also run CHKDSK to see if the root directory is full, or if some other problem is causing the error.

f

File is READ-ONLY

DESCRIPTION: You're trying to write over a read-only file when DOS tells you "no."

EXAMPLE: Karen must protect her work from co-workers who frequently need to use her data disks for their projects. So she uses the ATTRIB command to mark her files as read-only. Then, when she needs to change it herself, DOS won't let her because she's forgotten to remove the read-only attribute.

WHAT TO DO: To change or show the read-only attributes or other such characteristics of a file, you can use the ATTRIB command through its R option. For example, to set all of the .exe files on an entire floppy disk in the A: drive to read-only, you'd type

```
ATTRIB +R A:*.EXE
```

To clear this attribute, you'd type

```
ATTRIB -R A:*.EXE
```

File not found

DESCRIPTION: If you are trying to work with a file that you think exists, but which really doesn't exist (or exists, but just somewhere other than where you're looking), you'll get this message.

Actually, there are lots of ways to get this message. Deleting all the files (DEL *.*) in an already empty directory is one way; trying to TYPE a file that doesn't exist is another. It is also used by the DOS 4.x DOSSHELL as an equivalent to the DOS 5.0 DOSSHELL error message that tells you `The file doesn't exist.`

EXAMPLE: Jeff wants to copy a file named MYLET.DOC from the WORD directory to the NEWFILES directory. He carefully types in

```
copy MYLIT.DOC C:\NEWFILES
```

and gets the message `File not found.`

WHAT TO DO: Notice how MYLET.DOC turned into MYLIT.DOC. Double-check your work and retry the command, using the correct filename for the directory you're working from.

Format another (Y/N)?

DESCRIPTION: You'll see this prompt when you format a diskette. It requires a Y or N response—Y to format another diskette, and N to end the FORMAT program. Formatting is done to organize disks and diskettes so that the computer can locate and read information easily and quickly.

EXAMPLE: Jill wants to have some formatted diskettes handy for saving copies of files. She puts a blank diskette in drive B: and types

```
FORMAT b:
```

and she sees the message

```
Insert new diskette for drive B:

and press ENTER when ready...
```

The process takes a moment, and Jill can follow the activity on the screen. When the diskette has been formatted, the message `Format another (Y/N)?` appears.

WHAT TO DO: Press **Y** to format another diskette or **N** to end the FORMAT program.

f

General failure
(reading or writing)
drive x

G g

General failure (reading or writing) drive *x*

DESCRIPTION: As disks wear out, they can get bad spots that bring on this message. While these bad spots can have a variety of causes (such as bumping your PC accidentally during a disk read or write), there's only one effect: the spots cause parts of the disk to become unusable. You can't read from them or write to them once this happens. (This message will also appear in DOS 4.x when you're trying to read an unformatted diskette.) In the DOS Shell it's just `General Failure`.

Disk drives electronically record and play back data using the magnetic particles on the surface of a diskette. The files stored on your diskette are permanent unless you reformat the diskette, copy over with new files, or weaken the patterns of the magnetic particles by exposing the disk to magnetic fields (such as those surrounding magnetic tools). Then your files can become unreadable, resulting in this read error.

EXAMPLE: Steve brings home an important diskette from his office, and tacks it up on his refrigerator with a magnet so he won't forget to take it back to the office in the morning. Magnets, of course, mess up the magnetic particles on a disk. So when Steve pops the disk in his PC at work the next day, he gets the General failure message.

WHAT TO DO: Try pressing **F** for Fail first to avoid ending your application in the middle of a task. Then you can try **R** for Retry and **A** for Abort. Most likely, this message is telling you that all the data on your diskette is lost and not recoverable.

Help not available for
this command.

Help not available for this command.

DESCRIPTION: If you ask DOS 5.0's HELP for information about a nonexecutable DOS device driver (like ANSI.SYS) or a support file (like COMMAND.COM), you'll get this `Help not available` message. You'll also get it if you ask for help about a program that does not come with DOS.

DOS 6.0 comes with a much more extensive HELP program, which includes help about device drivers. If you try for a topic that's not covered in DOS 6.0, you'll get `Match not found` *and a list of available topics will appear.*

EXAMPLE: Tim uses DOS 5.0, and needs some help in figuring out how to change his CONFIG.SYS file. He types

```
HELP CONFIG.SYS
```

and gets the message `Help not available for this command`.

WHAT TO DO: DOS 5.0 won't give you on-line HELP for any non-executable DOS files. So if you have a question about something like AUTOEXEC.BAT, CONFIG.SYS, or ANSI.SYS, look it up in a DOS book.

HELP offers on-line syntax information on specific DOS commands including a description of the command, a list of switches and parameters, and a brief explanation of the actions of the switches and parameters. Say that you want to know more about the XCOPY command, you type

`HELP XCOPY`

and DOS tells you that XCOPY copies files (except hidden and system files) and directory trees. DOS also explains how to set up an XCOPY command, along with other details.

The DOS 5.0 version of HELP is still available in DOS 6.0, but it goes by a different name: DOSHELP. It provides the same level of help as if you had used the /? switch with the command—for example, DOSHELP XCOPY and XCOPY /? would both bring up the same help screen in DOS 6.0 HELP XCOPY would open the full DOS 6.0 Help program.

HMA not available : Loading DOS low

DESCRIPTION: You are trying to load DOS 5.0 or 6.0 into the HMA (high memory area) with the DOS=HIGH command in your CONFIG.SYS, but something won't let you. That something could be any of several different things. It could be that you don't have enough high memory, that it's not configured correctly, or that another program is already using the high memory area. Or, it could be that the lines of your CONFIG.SYS are not in the correct order.

EXAMPLE: Gloria has a friend named Bob who is quite the computer aficionado. Bob comes over to see Gloria, then spends the entire evening tinkering with her computer.

Bob thinks he'll do Gloria a favor and set up her CONFIG.SYS to load DOS into high memory. Using EDLIN, he adds the command DOS=HIGH as the first line of her computer's CONFIG.SYS file. After extolling the benefits of loading DOS high in a very confident and important tone, he is most embarrassed when DOS refuses to load itself into high memory and spits back this error message.

WHAT TO DO: Bob swallows his pride and gets out the DOS reference manual, which reminds him that HIMEM.SYS must be in the CONFIG.SYS file before the DOS=HIGH line. He adds the line

```
DEVICE=C:\DOS\HIMEM.SYS
```

to the CONFIG.SYS file, before the DOS=HIGH line. Gloria's CONFIG.SYS file now includes the following lines, in this order:

```
DEVICE=C:\DOS\HIMEM.SYS

DOS=HIGH
```

Bob types **MEM /C ¦ MORE** just to be sure (and to show Gloria how skillful he is with the pipe (¦) command). Gloria smiles indulgently.

With DOS 6.0, Bob could have typed MEM /C /P *instead of* MEM /C ¦ MORE. *Same result.*

If that hadn't worked, Bob could have tried these things:

- Type **MEM** to see if there is any extended memory available. If there's not, DOS can't load high. (Maybe Gloria has an XT with only 640K of memory!)

- Move the two lines (HIMEM.SYS and DOS=HIGH) to the beginning of the CONFIG.SYS file, if they're not already there.

Invalid drive specification

I i

Incorrect DOS version

DESCRIPTION: Some DOS commands will work only with particular versions of DOS. You'll get this message if a command requires a version of DOS that's different from the one you have loaded on your PC.

EXAMPLE: Pat just moved over to DOS 6.0 and is happy with many of DOS's new *utilities* (short programs that help her do PC housekeeping chores). Pat wants to share her newfound wealth, and transfers several of these helpful little programs to her friend's PC, which is still running under DOS 3.3. Alas! Most of these new utilities are designed to run only under DOS 6.0, and Pat's friend gets this Incorrect DOS version error message when she tries to run one of them.

WHAT TO DO: PC software is frequently upgraded. This means (among other things) that you should check with the manufacturer of your software to make sure it's compatible with the version of DOS you have on your computer. Also, it's always important to mail in your registration card so that you'll receive upgrade information. Upgrades bring new features and usually have a reduced purchase price.

In Pat's case, the new utility programs are new to DOS version 6.0; Pat's friend won't be able to use them until she also upgrades to DOS 6.0.

i

Incorrect parameter

See *Invalid parameter specifications.*

Insert disk with \COMMAND.COM in drive *x*
Press any key to continue. . .

DESCRIPTION: DOS is trying to reload the command processor and can't find it on the drive where DOS was started. This error message doesn't appear when you boot from a hard drive—only if you boot from a floppy.

EXAMPLE: Barry has an older system with two floppy drives. To boot his PC, he puts his system disk in drive A: and powers it on. He removes the system disk, inserts his word processing disk in A: and his data disk in B:, and loads the software. After he's done some word processing, Barry exits from the word processor and gets this message.

WHAT TO DO: To fix the problem, Barry simply needs to do what he's told—insert the DOS diskette in drive A: and press any key.

If, like Barry, you've booted your PC off a floppy, you'll have to stick the COMMAND.COM disk back into the drive (because DOS usually looks for COMMAND.COM in the last place it was found).

Working in a two-floppy-drive world can have its moments. When you start your system from a bootable floppy that you've created, COMMAND.COM has been copied onto your diskette. This is a program that reads the commands you enter at the DOS prompt.

When you're done with one program and want to move on to the next, your PC returns to and loads the COMMAND.COM file, so it will know how to handle your next command-line instruction.

Insufficient disk space

DESCRIPTION: Your diskette or fixed drive doesn't have enough free space to hold the file being written.

EXAMPLE: Joe keeps copies of his word processing files on a floppy disk. He has a lot of files, and his disk is filling up. He tries to copy just one more file on the diskette and gets this message.

WHAT TO DO: Time to format another data diskette! You can run CHKDSK to check the status of the disk if you think there's still room to spare. If it's your hard disk that's full, you can always take off some of the programs or data files that aren't needed as urgently.

You may also benefit from using a zip program like PKZIP (which you should be able to purchase through any PC user group), or you can buy a data compression program like Stacker.

Insufficient memory

DESCRIPTION: "I'm tryin' to think, but nuthin' happens!" Your PC is clearly telling you it doesn't have the oomph to handle your last command.

EXAMPLE: Sally has an XT with 640K (kilobytes) of RAM. She tries to load a new piece of software she's just purchased and gets this Insufficient memory message. The new software requires only 512K of free RAM, but Sally discovers that she has so many TSRs and device drivers loaded that her PC's free conventional memory is less than what's required.

TSR stands for terminate-and-stay-resident. When you run a TSR program, it immediately "goes to sleep," hiding in the background until you press a certain key combination. Then it pops up, does

its thing, and disappears again. TSRs are normally loaded in one's
AUTOEXEC.BAT file.

A device driver is a system-level program that controls an input or
output device, such as a mouse or a scanner. Device drivers are
normally loaded in the CONFIG.SYS file.

WHAT TO DO: Sally removes several of her TSRs, and the new
software runs just fine. She needs to keep her PC's free, conventional memory (RAM) clear if she wants to run most software,
since her PC loads these "extras" in the same space that her programs need to run.

If Sally had a 386 or 486 computer and DOS 5.0 or above, it
would be a different story. With that setup, she could load those
drivers and TSRs out of the way, so they're still available but don't
eat up the valuable space in conventional memory.

The DOS files that perform these memory management tricks are
HIMEM.SYS and EMM386.EXE. You can learn more about them
in your DOS manual, or from the on-line HELP command if you
have DOS 6.0.

Internal stack overflow
System halted

DESCRIPTION: When the modem, mouse, keyboard, and printer start sending signals, DOS gets fed up with all the interruptions and cries Stop! This message is sometimes worded as simply Stack overflow.

Each time you press a key, the keyboard generates a hardware interrupt or signal for attention. Your computer's peripherals (like printers, mice, modems, etc.) are always interrupting the central processing unit, vying for its attention.

Each time your PC's CPU is interrupted, it tries to store the information it was acting upon in a special area (reserved in conventional memory) called a stack. If the interruptions start building, this stack overflows—and now you have a problem. If your PC "blows its stack," it's because your programs and DOS—while trying to juggle the quick series of signals coming from printers, mice, modems, and the rest of the Peripherals Gang—have exhausted the stack.

EXAMPLE: Julie's computer is hooked up to a lot of toys—a scanner, a mouse, a monitor, a joystick, two printers, a tape backup, a CD-ROM, and a modem. (Julie likes to live life to the hilt.)

Onc day, Julic is proccssing away at several tasks simultaneously, when the screen goes blank and her PC spits out `Internal stack overflow`.

WHAT TO DO: Try turning your PC off and on again. A soft boot won't work; you're really going to have to power off. (Make sure you wait a few seconds before you turn the power on again.)

If you're experiencing frequent stack overflows, you can increase the possible number of stacks by changing the CONFIG.SYS file. For example, try STACKS=9,256.

The size of the stacks can be specified as 0, or between 32 and 512 bytes. The number of stacks can be specified as 0, or between 8 and 64. Usually, it's more effective to increase the number rather than the size.

Invalid characters in volume label

DESCRIPTION: You're receiving this error message because you tried to name a volume label and didn't follow the rules.

EXAMPLE: Gloria likes to give her disk labels funny little names. One rainy day, to label a spreadsheet data disk in drive A:, she types

```
LABEL A:* /\ *
```

explaining that the file was for her bookkeeper who has a sharp nose and peculiar eyes. This is much too much for DOS, and Gloria gets an error message.

WHAT TO DO: The rules are clear. You get 11 characters maximum, including spaces, and you cannot use any of these characters

```
* ? / \ ¦ . , ; : + = [ ]
```

Give helpful, descriptive names to disk labels. Gloria's spreadsheet disk could be named something practical like SNOZ&EYZ_93.

Invalid COMMAND.COM

DESCRIPTION: You'll get this message after leaving an application. This is not good. But it can be fixed. Somehow

COMMAND.COM, a very important file, has been damaged or erased from your system diskette or fixed drive.

EXAMPLE: While other people are cooking dinner, Fred's home, cookin' with DOS! More power is used during dinner hours, however—and since Fred's office is in a residential area, the power coming into his office fluctuates during these peak times.

A little surge of power, and Fred sees this message as his PC locks up.

WHAT TO DO: Nobody would intentionally remove your COMMAND.COM file, would they? If you get this message, you can assume that power fluctuations are altering COMMAND.COM or that a batch file is erasing it.

Try to restart your PC from a diskette and then copy COMMAND.COM to your root directory or to wherever your SHELL directive guides you.

If you believe that a batch file is erasing or altering this file, edit the file. If a program is erasing it, get hold of the person who sold you the software.

As for Fred, he needs to check out purchasing a *surge suppressor.* It's an inexpensive electrical apparatus that prevents high-voltage surges from damaging a PC's circuitry.

i

DESCRIPTION: This is a minor problem that you can wash your hands of very quickly. You were booting or changing the date and were asked to enter a new date. You either gave DOS an invalid date or you messed up when separating the days, month, and year (you used commas instead of periods, or colons instead of slashes).

EXAMPLE: Karen hears horrific tales that a computer virus might activate worldwide on Cinco de Mayo. Karen hasn't practiced safe computing; for years she's used other peoples' disks indiscriminately and figures she'd better do something—just in case her PC has been infected! Karen sets her PC's date back two days and makes a note to set the date forward to the correct date (once May 5th has passed). Karen simply types DATE at the command prompt and gets this message

```
Current date is Wed 05-04-1993
Enter new date (mm-dd-yy):
```

To change this date (she'd keep the present date by pressing Enter), Karen types in her new date

```
05-02-93
```

separating the month, day, and year with hyphens. Then, on May 6 (which appears on her PC as May 4), Karen cleverly resets the date by typing

```
05>06>93
```

But Karen is using the wrong symbol (>) to separate the date information and she gets the `Invalid date` message.

WHAT TO DO: Type in dates properly, separating months, days, and years with hyphens, slashes, or periods, and you won't get this error message. By the way, number months from 1 through 12. Number days from 1 through 31. Give two numbers for years, 80 through 99, or give four numbers for 1980 through 2099. If you want to display dates in European formats, year-month-day, or day-month-year, use the COUNTRY command in the CONFIG.SYS file.

Invalid directory

DESCRIPTION: Piece of cake. You've either given DOS the name of a directory that doesn't exist, misspelled the directory name, or messed up on the path.

EXAMPLE: Jack has taken some PC classes, and he's set up nested directories. He wants to work on a file in a directory named CARS that is contained in his WORD directory.

At the root directory, he types cd\word and gets the prompt for the WORD subdirectory:

```
C:\WORD>
```

He tries to move into CARS by typing cd\cars and gets the Invalid directory message. Jack looks in his notes and comes up with his CARS directory by typing cd\auto\cars, and he's a happy man!

WHAT TO DO: Check out your directory names and make sure they exist. Try the command again. Make sure your path is given correctly.

Invalid drive in search path

DESCRIPTION: One of the entries in your PATH statement has an invalid disk drive name. The disk drive may not exist, or it may have been temporarily hidden by a SUBST or JOIN command.

EXAMPLE: Dianna made some modifications to her PATH command in her AUTOEXEC.BAT file and accidentally typed in a D: instead of a C: for the location of her word processor. Later when she executed a command, she saw this message on her screen.

WHAT TO DO: Dianna can use the PATH command to check the path for errors. If she finds the mistake, she can use EDIT or EDLIN to correct the problem. By just typing

PATH

at the DOS prompt and pressing **Enter**, she sees

```
PATH=C:\EXCEL;D:\;C:\DOS;
```
and knows she must use EDIT or EDLIN to change the D after EXCEL to a C.

Invalid drive specification

DESCRIPTION: You've simply given the wrong letter when specifying a drive.

If this message is followed by *Specified drive does not exist or is non-removable*, you are probably trying to specify a drive that is not suitable for a particular command. Turn to the "S" part of the book and look up that message to learn more.

EXAMPLE: Susan wants to switch over from the C: drive to the A: drive. Her cat bumps her arm, and she accidently types in

    q:

and her PC retorts

    Invalid drive specification

Susan tries again, typing a: instead, and all ends well.

WHAT TO DO: Try not to mess up when you're typing something important, or even when it isn't important.

Invalid environment size specified

See *Parameter value not in allowed range.*

Invalid file name or file not found

DESCRIPTION: You tried to use wild-card characters with the TYPE command, and DOS wouldn't let you.

EXAMPLE: Jeff has several files named AUTOEXEC, each with different extensions, that various installation programs have created. Jeff wants to look at all of these files, and he thinks he'll save time and be clever by using a wild-card so that each file will be typed onto the screen consecutively. He types in

```
type AUTOEXEC.*
```

and presses Enter. The *, substituted for the file extensions, accounts for the error message that follows.

WHAT TO DO: Don't use wild cards with the TYPE command.

Invalid media or Track 0 Bad - disk unusable
Format Terminated
Format another (Y/N)?

DESCRIPTION: You're trying to format a disk to have a capacity that it wasn't intended to have. Or, the diskette is truly defective.

EXAMPLE: Denzil wants to format a low density 3 1/2-inch diskette in a high-density drive. He knows that he has to specify the /F720 switch with the FORMAT command, and he does so. But when reaching for the disk to be formatted, he accidentally grabs a high-density diskette. Seconds into the formatting process, DOS comes back with this message.

WHAT TO DO: High-density 5 1/4-inch diskettes are great— you can format them as either 1.2MB or 360K. Whichever capacity you need, you're covered. This is not the case with 3 1/2-inch diskettes, though. Low density must be formatted *only* as low density, and high density only as high density. You're right, it's not fair, but that's the way it is.

If you check the capacity on the diskette and the drive, and everything seems like it should work, maybe the diskette is defective. If so, send it to the manufacturer for a refund.

Invalid number of parameters

See *Required parameter missing.*

Invalid parameter

An alternate version of *Invalid parameter specifications.* You might get this version, for example, if you typed in

```
JOIN A:
```

because you did not specify the second drive, which is required.

Invalid parameter specifications

DESCRIPTION: At least one of the parameters you've typed in for a command is not correct. This message also appears as Incorrect parameter or Invalid parameter.

EXAMPLE: Jim, using DOS 5.0, is cleaning up his directories. He types

```
UNDELETE *.BAK /KEEP
```

and the screen responds with the message

```
Invalid parameter specifications
```

because /KEEP is not a valid parameter.

WHAT TO DO: Use some care when keying in required information such as colons after disk drive letters, or when spacing before and after switches. Messages under the individual commands will often give more specific information. Later versions of DOS give you more latitude. With DOS 5.0 and 6.0, you can type **HELP**—followed by a command name—and you'll get a listing of the correct way to write the command (its *syntax*). This is really helpful if you've forgotten the required or optional switches and parameters.

Invalid partition table

i

DESCRIPTION: If your hard drive is very large, you might *partition* it into smaller, more manageable chunks. For instance, your drive might be divided into C: and D:. (Hard disks larger than 32MB *had* to be partitioned with DOS versions prior to 4.0).

If, during startup from the fixed drive, DOS detects any invalid information in the information you're using to create the partition, you'll see this error message.

EXAMPLE: Jack wants to divide his fixed drive—half for DOS and half for another operating system. First, he makes an emergency boot disk, and backs up all of his drives. (Jack is no fool.)

Once the boot disk is ready and the drives are backed up, Jack creates the partitions. But when he attempts to reboot DOS from the hard disk, DOS finds a problem in the hard disk's partition information.

WHAT TO DO: Jack must restart DOS from his emergency boot disk. If he has a DOS version 4.0 or above, he can run FDISK to examine, and possibly correct, the fixed disk's partition information. (FDISK is not available with DOS 3.x. He would use ASGNPART with DOS 3.2, or PART with DOS 3.3.) He may have to rebuild the partition table using the UNFORMAT / PARTN command. The file PARTNSAV.FIL should be on Jack's emergency boot disk.

i

Invalid Path

See *Path not found.*

Invalid path, not directory, or directory not empty

DESCRIPTION: Relax. This is one of those easy-to-resolve dilemmas. You're trying to remove a current directory that isn't empty or doesn't exist. (The DOS gods have special ways of protecting you from yourself.) You'll also get this message if you try to delete a file using the RD command.

EXAMPLE: Juanita wants to get rid of her directory that holds Christmas projects (named XMAS). She goes to her root directory and gives the command

    RD XMAS

and her computer responds `Invalid path, not directory or directory not empty`. So Juanita types

    CD\XMAS

to move to the directory, where she deletes all of the Christmas files (**DEL *.***). Then she is able to go back out to the root directory and finally remove XMAS.

WHAT TO DO: You must delete any files or remove any subdirectories in a directory before it can be removed.

i

Invalid switch

DESCRIPTION: Did you ever go into a dark room, find a light switch, flick it on—and nothing happened? It was probably a switch that belonged to another room. Or else you need a new electrician.

If DOS gives you an `Invalid switch` message, it's because you've typed in a command and have indicated a nonexistent (or duplicate) switch for that command.

EXAMPLE: Jay is getting ready to use his word processor, and wants to get into a subdirectory entitled LETTERS. He types in

```
C:\CD/WORD/LETTERS
```

and presses Enter. But he gets an `Invalid switch` error message because he's used the wrong slashes—the *forward* slash (/) instead of the *backslash* (\)—in his command.

WHAT TO DO: If you get this message, double-check your entries to see if your switches are correct. You can also get help in DOS 5.0 and 6.0 by typing **HELP** *command* and then retyping your command with the corrections.

i

*Memory allocation error
Cannot load MS-DOS,
system halted*

Memory allocation error
Cannot load MS-DOS, system halted

DESCRIPTION: This is a lobotomy alert—somehow a program has messed with the area where DOS keeps track of available memory.

EXAMPLE: Mark likes to run "beta" programs—test software—for a software development company. Sometimes things just happen, and a test program will "blow up" (that is, it'll either kick Mark back out to the DOS prompt or it'll freeze up and refuse to continue). Sometimes the beta programs will confuse DOS so badly that it will report a `Memory allocation error`.

m

WHAT TO DO: Mark should just restart DOS. It's not as bad as it sounds. If the error persists, and he's booting from a floppy disk, he could make a new copy of the MS-DOS diskette from his system diskette. If he's booting from a hard disk, he could use the SYS command to transfer a new copy of the system to his disk.

In Mark's case, he expects trouble since he's running beta software. If you get this message repeatedly for no apparent reason, and recopying the system files does not help, you might have a hardware problem.

No paper error writing device PRN Abort, Retry, Ignore, Fail?

No free file handles
Cannot start COMMAND.COM, exiting

DESCRIPTION: Your PC tries to load a second copy of the command processor, but too many files are already open.

EXAMPLE: Sara is using software that lets her shell out to DOS, but all her file handles are in use by the application itself, so she gets this message. Sara knows that she can usually leave this software to work in DOS, because there's a special option on the menu that says "DOS commands."

File handles are nicknames or token numbers DOS uses to refer to an open file. You can change the number of file handles available with the FILES= command in CONFIG.SYS.

WHAT TO DO: Try rebooting the system. If this doesn't work, you'll need to increase the number of files in the FILES= statement in the CONFIG.SYS file, and then restart DOS. Setting FILES= to 30 or 40 is usually sufficient for any application.

n

No paper error writing device PRN
Abort, Retry, Ignore, Fail?

See *Printer out of paper error writing device LPT1.*

No Path

DESCRIPTION: The PATH command allows you to access files from one directory while you're in another directory. Normally you can find out what directories have been set up as a path by typing PATH at the DOS prompt. The path is normally set up in the AUTOEXEC.BAT file. If no path has been set up, you'll get the No Path error message.

EXAMPLE: Laura just took a class in DOS and she's having a lot of fun trying out new things on her PC. Good for Laura! She somehow removes her path statement line from the AUTOEXEC.BAT file, and when she reboots she finds that DOS can't locate any of the DOS commands unless she's actually in the DOS directory!

Puzzled, she types PATH at the DOS prompt to make sure that her path statement includes the DOS directory. But since the entire path line was deleted from the AUTOEXEC.BAT file, there *is* no path, and DOS, quite appropriately, reports No Path.

n

WHAT TO DO: Laura needs to get the path statement back in the AUTOEXEC.BAT file. The best way would be to copy the backup AUTOEXEC file over the top of the modified one, with this command:

```
COPY AUTOEXEC.BAK AUTOEXEC.BAT
```

If the path in your AUTOEXEC.BAT file seems intact, you may have accidentally typed PATH: while playing around. This would cancel the path in memory. If this happens, it's easiest just to reboot and let AUTOEXEC.BAT reset it when it executes.

No room for system on destination disk

DESCRIPTION: Your destination disk doesn't have the required reserved space available for the DOS system files, so the system can't be transferred to the diskette. System files are picky! They want enough room *in the right place* on your diskettes.

EXAMPLE: Greg wants to turn his floppy disk into a system disk. He tries to transfer system files to the diskette using the DOS command SYS A, and gets this message because his diskette doesn't have enough room (in the right places) for the special hidden DOS files.

WHAT TO DO: In this instance, Greg can start over by simply deleting all files on his diskette and then retrying the SYS command.

No room in directory for file

n

DESCRIPTION: This message tells you basically the same thing as Cannot make directory entry, except it occurs while using EDLIN. Go read the *Cannot make directory entry* section, then come back here.

Are you back? Good. As you just learned from reading, a disk's root directory can contain only a fixed number of entries. (An entry is either a directory or a file. The root directory can contain any combination of them.)

If your root directory contains the maximum number of entries it can contain, and you try to edit a file with EDLIN, you will be told No room in directory for file.

Here's the reason: When you edit a file with EDLIN, it automatically saves the old version of the file with an identical file name and the BAK extension. If DOS created that BAK file, the maximum

number of directory entries would be exceeded. Therefore, DOS won't even let you enter the EDLIN program.

WHAT TO DO: Delete some files from the root directory, then try again. For example, you could type **DEL** `*`.**BAK** to get rid of the existing backup files.

Non-System disk or disk error
Replace and strike any key when ready

n

DESCRIPTION: The diskette you're trying to boot from isn't a system disk. (This message will also appear if you try to run FOR-MAT /S or SYS from a non-system disk.) Depending on the DOS version, the message might tell you to "press" any key instead of "strike," but the meaning is the same.

Some other variations you might see, depending on how the disk was formatted, include:

```
This disk can't boot:  it was formatted by CP Backup
Change disks and press a key

Non System Diskette
MS-DOS backup diskette
```

```
Replace and press any ken when ready. . .

This disk is not bootable
```

The solution is the same regardless of the wording.

EXAMPLE: Jay has a PC with two floppy drives, and he wants to boot his PC from the disk that also contains his word processor. When he puts his program diskette into drive A: and boots up, he gets this non-system disk message.

WHAT TO DO: Jay can use the SYS command to move DOS onto his program disk. Certain locations, or sectors, must be free to hold the system files. If these locations have already been taken, Jay must start from scratch by formatting a new system diskette, copying DOS onto it, and then copying over the word processor.

DOS's system files camp out on your hard drive and all other boot disks. DOS system files consist of three files; two of them are "invisible," or hidden. If you use DIR, you'll never see these secret files listed. COMMAND.COM is the third file, and you'll see it in your directory listing. All three of these files make up the stuff of DOS, or your PC's operating system. When you use **SYS** *or* **FORMAT** * /***S***, these files are copied to the appropriate locations to make the disk bootable.*

Not enough free memory to run xxxxxx.

DESCRIPTION: Your PC doesn't have enough free random access memory (RAM) to run a particular program or command.

EXAMPLE: Blair enjoys several special programs that are always available to her. She can press a special key for a pop-up calendar, special sounds, and some other fun stuff. These programs, called *TSRs*, are loaded into her PC's memory at startup and stay there, waiting for action.

Blair always checks the memory requirements when she purchases new software—so she's surprised when Not enough free memory to run WordPerfect appears as she's loading the newest version of WordPerfect.

WHAT TO DO: Memory-resident programs (like Blair's calendar) are called TSRs because they load, *Terminate*, and *Stay Resident*. Some folks refer to them, however, as TCPs—for Terminate and Cause Problems. That's a bit rough, but if you have trouble loading new software, you can try running the software without loading any TSRs beforehand. You can simply not type in the command to run the TSR—or, if the TSRs are loaded from your AUTOEXEC.BAT file, use a bootable disk to start your PC from drive A:.

n

You can also copy your AUTOEXEC.BAT file to AUTOEXEC.SAV and then delete all the TSR lines from the AUTOEXEC.BAT and reboot. Then, when you want the TSRs back, simply copy AUTOEXEC.SAV to AUTOEXEC.BAT again!

Not enough memory

n

This message may appear with or without the second line, `Operation cannot be completed`. See *Not enough free memory to run xxxxxx*.

Not ready error writing device PRN
Abort, Retry, Ignore, Fail?

See *Printer out of paper error writing device LPT1*.

Not ready reading drive x
Abort, Retry, Fail?

DESCRIPTION: Your PC's printer or drive (or another device) is telling you that it's not ready to receive or send data.

EXAMPLE: Kelly wants to copy a data file to a diskette in drive B:. From the C prompt, she types in

```
copy MYF.DOC b:
```

and gets this message because she's forgotten to put a diskette in the B: drive.

WHAT TO DO: This message usually appears if you're tying to access a device, such as a floppy drive, which isn't ready to receive data. It's a good idea to always check the floppy drive. You might have forgotten to put in the diskette, or the drive door might still be open.

n

Out of environment space

Out of environment space

DESCRIPTION: DOS has run out of space in a reserved area of memory called the environment. DOS uses this space to track small but important pieces of information that help your PC run faster and perform better, including information used in setting the PATH, PROMPT, TEMP and some related areas. Think of the environment as sort of a scratch pad. In this case, the scratch pad is full!

EXAMPLE: Harold has a hard time keeping track of the date, so he decides to enlist the help of his PC. Harold modifies the prompt line in his AUTOEXEC.BAT file like this:

```
SET PROMPT=$D $P$G
```

which makes his PC's prompt look like this:

```
Thu 06-18-1993 C:\>
```

DOS has a role in Harold's prompt customization, creating something called a PROMPT envar and setting this envar to hold the value of $D PG. Any time the prompt is displayed on Harold's PC, this PROMPT envar has been read.

This little story ends well. Harold now knows the date whenever he's asked. But if Harold already had a lot of software on his PC (including TSRs, or those cute little programs like calendars that stay resident in random access memory even when they aren't running), things might have ended differently, with Harold getting the Out of environment space message when he tried to increase the size of his prompt.

WHAT TO DO: When DOS starts a program, including a TSR, it hands out a copy of the current environment to the program which, in turn, can use those variables as it wants. It can take away some variables and add others—in its own copy of the environment. When the program ends, DOS gets rid of this copy and brings back the real environment.

Before DOS 5.0, the environment space was limited to about 160 bytes. With DOS 5.0, the default size was increased to 256 bytes. Still, if you have a long system path and a bunch of envars, you could still see the Out of environment space message.

You can increase the size of the environment by putting the following in your CONFIG.SYS file:

    COMMAND /E:xxxxx

which sets the amount of memory in bytes for the DOS environment. The size can range up to 32,768 bytes.

Packed file is corrupt

DESCRIPTION: First of all, don't panic. This message has a bark bigger than its bite. Nothing has been corrupted! You're probably working on a 286, 386, or 486 processor and have moved DOS into the high memory area (HMA). Loading DOS high frees up some conventional memory blocks that older programs aren't expecting to be available, and some programs get confused by it.

Versions of DOS before 5.0 used to reserve the first 64K of memory for their own use. Programmers began to get used to this particular block of memory being unavailable to them, and they wrote programs that assumed it wouldn't be open.

DOS 5.0, however, changed all that. DOS versions 5.0 and above come with the ability to load themselves into high memory, freeing up this long-unavailable 64K. Some applications programs don't understand what's happening when they find themselves in these uncharted memory regions (addresses). And so this error message flashes on your screen.

WHAT TO DO: Piece of pastry. A special command was invented to handle this generational confusion. Let's say you want to run a program named taxman.exe. Type

```
LOADFIX taxman.exe
```

The LOADFIX command loads a confused program above the first segment of memory. It's a simple fix.

Parameter format not correct

DESCRIPTION: This means that you've probably messed up a few slashes here or there when you were giving a command. Easy to fix.

EXAMPLE: Lorraine wants to format a system diskette in drive A:. She types

```
FORMAT a:s
```

and gets this error message. Then she double-checks her DOS book and retypes

```
FORMAT a:/s
```

and it works.

WHAT TO DO: First, make sure that you understand the command you're trying to use. You can look it up in a DOS book if you're shaky. In DOS 5.0 or 6.0, to see a quick reminder of how commands work, type HELP and the name of the command to see the command's syntax. For instance, if you want help with the FORMAT command, just type

```
HELP format
```

and you'll get help from DOS. When you see the problem, simply reissue your command.

Parameter value not in allowed range

DESCRIPTION: So you're going techie on us—good for you! You were trying to add space to your system's DOS environment and got this message instead.

EXAMPLE: Lou Ann has a lot of applications on her system, so she's built some hefty paths. Now she wants to accommodate her PC's need for more DOS space by changing the size of its DOS environment.

All Lou Ann needs to do is change her CONFIG.SYS file with a line that gives an actual size of the DOS environment (something in the range of 160 through 32,768 bytes). In this case, the value she gives for this range isn't valid, and Lou Ann gets this Parameter value not in allowed range message on her screen.

WHAT TO DO: Take a good look at the CONFIG.SYS file, and make sure that what you typed in the /E switch of COMMAND.COM is really a number from 160 to 32,768. Once you edit CONFIG.SYS, reboot, and you'll probably be just fine.

Path not found

DESCRIPTION: DOS has asked you to specify a path during some operation it's performing (like BACKUP, XCOPY, RESTORE, or others), and you've given faulty information. You probably made a typo!

EXAMPLE: Julie is backing up the files in her WORD directory using the BACKUP command. When she issues the command to start the backup, she types

```
BACKUP C:\WORS\*.* A:
```

Since she typed WORS instead of WORD, DOS can't find the path to the files, and it reports Path not found.

WHAT TO DO: Julie should make sure that the directory she is specifying really exists. If it does, she probably forgot to include a backslash or a drive letter.

Printer out of paper error writing device LPT1: Abort, Retry, Ignore, Fail?

See *Printer out of paper error writing device PRN.*

Printer out of paper error writing device PRN Abort, Retry, Ignore, Fail?

DESCRIPTION: Your printer is out of paper.

EXAMPLE: Lisa likes to print out copies of special batch files to keep for her records. To keep a copy of MENU.BAT she types

```
type MENU.BAT>prn
```

and she gets this message:

```
Printer out of paper error writing device PRN
Abort, Retry, Ignore, Fail?
```

because the printer is out of paper.

WHAT TO DO: Just reload the printer with paper and press R for Retry.

Program too big to fit in memory

DESCRIPTION: This message can be deceiving. It's possible that the program is probably too large, and you will not be able to run it without adding more memory or freeing up some existing resources (see *Not enough free memory to run xxxxx*). If you're running a BASIC program, this is almost certainly the answer.

But if you're not running BASIC and you get this message with a program that you've run successfully before, then perhaps some stray bits of a program are lurking in memory, tying up your resources.

EXAMPLE: Cindy turns her computer on in the morning, works on it all day, and turns it off at night. During the course of a day, she runs all kinds of programs—spreadsheets, utilities, beta (test) versions of games, environments like Microsoft Windows, and word processing programs.

Just before quitting time, Cindy decides to use WordPerfect to type a quick note to her boss. When she types the command to start the program, she gets the message `Program too big to fit in memory`. This has to be a mistake, she thinks, because WordPerfect fit into memory just fine several hours ago!

WHAT TO DO: Reboot your computer. When Cindy reboots, all the quirky little program fragments that had been left over in her computer's memory from her daily activities are dumped out, and the computer starts over with a clear memory.

Rebooting nearly always solves this problem. If you continue to get the message, run CHKDSK /F to make sure that all is well with your computer's file structure. (Of course, there's always the chance that the program truly is too big for your computer, especially if you have less than 640K of RAM.)

If you still get the message, try the solutions listed under *Not enough free memory to run xxxxx.*

p

Read error on source drive

See *Source diskette bad or incompatible.*

Read fault error reading drive *x*
Abort, Retry, Fail?

DESCRIPTION: Your PC can't read data from the designated drive.

EXAMPLE: Todd promises Liz he'll print her word-processed data file if she'll give him her diskette. Todd wants to impress Liz, so you can imagine his frustration when he puts the diskette into his floppy drive, tries to read her file, and gets this error message on his screen.

WHAT TO DO: Todd can try pressing **R** for Retry. If this doesn't do it, he can try reinserting the disk and pressing **R** again. If he still has no luck, the disk might be damaged; if it's the only copy of the data, Todd may need to find a friend who is very knowledgeable and has some special software to recover the data. Otherwise, he could ask Liz to recopy the file onto a different floppy disk and try again.

Yet, because the diskette is from Liz's system (and not Todd's), the problem might be that Liz's drive is out of alignment and needs repair (or Todd's drive may have developed a mechanical problem). Anyway, this whole mess provides Todd an opportunity to ask Liz out for dinner to discuss . . . the importance of backups!

Required parameter missing

DESCRIPTION: You're still an okay person, but when you typed a command, you simply left out some information that DOS needs in order to do what you want it to do.

EXAMPLE: Tyrone wants to get rid of a subdirectory. At the root (C:\>), he types in RD without naming a directory for the command to delete—and this error message appears. Relax, Tyrone. This is fixable.

WHAT TO DO: Often, DOS insists that you include a parameter (information that specifies) when you give a command. Here, you've got to tell DOS the name of the directory before the directory can be removed.

In DOS 5.0 or 6.0, you can type **HELP RD** and DOS will provide some assistance. Here's what you would see in DOS 5.0:

```
Removes (deletes) a directory.
RMDIR [drive:]path
RD [drive:]path
```

In DOS 6.0, you would get a much more detailed and lengthy explanation.

You can use HELP in conjunction with any command to get a reminder of the command's syntax (precisely how a command should be stated to DOS). You can also type **HELP** *by itself to get a listing of all DOS commands available. This works in both DOS 5.0 and DOS 6.0, but you'll get a much more detailed explanation with DOS 6.0.*

r

System transferred

Sector not found
Abort, Retry, Fail?

DESCRIPTION: DOS can't read what you've stored on your disk or fixed drive; this could be due to physical damage to the disk or drive, mechanical misalignment of the special equipment inside your PC, or stress to your PC's drive, over time. Maybe DOS can't read the first track on your disk (track 0, called the boot record), which must be read before DOS can be loaded into your PC's memory.

EXAMPLE: Jim tries to read a file from his floppy diskette, and gets this error message. Jim closes his eyes and tries again by pressing R for retry. It works! (Well, sometimes it works. Other times you have to give up and press A for Abort.)

S

What is a sector? Well, as you probably already know, you have to format a disk before DOS can store your data on it. DOS first does a low-level format to create magnetic patterns called tracks and sectors; these block off the storage areas DOS uses to read and write data.

WHAT TO DO: If retrying the command doesn't work, then you'd better copy as many files as you can to another diskette.

Most hard disks will have some bad sectors. If it becomes necessary, you can find the bad sectors, retrieve the data, and mark them as bad, using special third-party utility software. This prevents other programs from using the same sector and allows you to keep using your hard disk.

Seek error
Abort, Retry, Fail?

S

DESCRIPTION: DOS just can't find the file on your disk you were asking for. There might be a real (physical) tracking problem with your drive.

EXAMPLE: Jane puts a diskette in drive B: and gets this error when she tries to bring up a file.

WHAT TO DO: You can always hope that your disk simply needs to be reinserted into the drive. Easy fix. If you keep getting this error, try putting your disk in another disk drive to see if you can pull up the file. If this works, your PC's floppy drive probably needs to be repaired or adjusted.

DESCRIPTION: You're running a program like Windows, which supports file sharing, without having first run DOS's SHARE.EXE. Or, you're running a program on a network that tries to access a file another program is currently using.

EXAMPLE: Gene just purchased windowing software for his PC. This is a graphical user interface, or GUI (pronounced gooey!), that will let him work with multiple on-screen windows. At the same time, the GUI acts as an intermediary between DOS and Gene's word processor, spreadsheet, and other software applications. Gene installs his program and it seems to run okay, but when he tries to use several programs at once, he gets this message.

WHAT TO DO: Running a program like Gene's windowing software requires that SHARE.EXE be installed through the AUTOEXEC.BAT file. Specific instructions should be included with the software documentation. You'll use a text editor, such as EDLIN (or EDIT if you have DOS 5.0 or above), to make this change. If you feel squeamish, ask for help from a member of a PC user group or from a DOS-literate friend.

S

Here's one for the "go figure" files. Once in a while you may get a `Sharing violation` *error when you already have SHARE.EXE loaded. In this case, unloading SHARE.EXE from memory (taking its line out of your AUTOEXEC.BAT and rebooting) may solve the problem. Technically this shouldn't work, but it sometimes does.*

Source diskette bad or incompatible
Copy process ended
Copy another diskette (Y/N)?

See *Drive types or diskette types not compatible.*

Specified drive does not exist or is non-removable

DESCRIPTION: This message is usually preceded by *Invalid drive specification.* You're trying to use DISKCOMP or DISKCOPY when one of the floppy drives in your command either doesn't exist or is a hard drive.

(The message for an invalid drive specification is `Drive not ready - cannot continue` in DOS 3.x; for an attempt to specify a hard drive, the message is `Cannot diskcopy hard disk media`.)

EXAMPLE: Serena wants to copy a floppy disk. She puts the source diskette in A:, and the destination in B:, and accidentally types

```
DISKCOPY A: C:
```

and she receives this error message.

WHAT TO DO: Commands like DISKCOMP and DISKCOPY work only with floppy drives. You need to change your last command to include two valid floppy disk drive letters, such as

```
DISKCOPY A: B:
```

If you just have one floppy drive, or mismatched drives, you can use the same drive as source and destination, using the command

```
DISKCOPY A: A:
```

In this case the source and destination drives are the same—and DOS lets you give the same drive as both the source and target.

S

Stack overflow

See *Internal stack overflow.*

Syntax error

DESCRIPTION: If you're working in an early version of DOS and make a slight error when entering a DOS command, you can get this message. It can appear if you leave out some information, give extra information, put extra space in a file or path name, or use an incorrect switch.

You also get this message if you type the wrong command while using EDLIN with any version of DOS.

EXAMPLE: Allison's working in DOS 3.1 and wants to use the FIND command to search for data. She forgets to enclose the date in quotes and gets this message.

WHAT TO DO: Take a good look at the command you gave, making sure you've used the right parameters and typed everything correctly. You'll need to find the mistake and then retype.

S

Target cannot be used for backup
Abort, Retry, Fail?

DESCRIPTION: Your target diskette when using BACKUP in DOS 5.0 or below might have a format that is unrecognizable, or is simply a bad diskette.

DOS 6.0 comes with a different program, MSBACKUP, instead of BACKUP. Unlike BACKUP, which is an ordinary DOS command, MSBACKUP is a full-fledged application, with its own graphical interface.

EXAMPLE: Quinton, a DOS 5.0 user, wants to make a backup of his fixed drive—just in case. When he is backing up his files, one of the diskettes Quinton inserts is defective. DOS can't write Quinton's files to this disk in its present state, and it lets him know. So Quinton inserts another diskette and continues the backup.

WHAT TO DO: Have extra disks handy during a BACKUP in case this happens. Later, you can run CHKDSK on the bad diskette to see if there are bad sectors. Either toss the diskette, ask for your money back, or (only if you have DOS 5.0!) reformat it with the FORMAT /U command. (The /U switch formats each sector "unconditionally.")

TARGET diskette bad or incompatible

DESCRIPTION: You're duplicating a disk with DISKCOPY, and DOS runs into a destination disk (target) that uses a lower-density format than the source disk.

EXAMPLE: Julio has two computers—one at home (with two 360K floppy drives), and one at work (with a 1.2MB drive and a 1.44MB drive). If he's not careful, Julio can have some problems working between the systems due to formatting differences.

At work, Julio needs to make a copy of one of his diskettes using DISKCOPY. He places a 360K diskette—formatted at home—in drive B:, and places his original diskette—a 1.2MB one—in drive A:. Then Julio types

```
DISKCOPY A: B:
```

But having a destination disk with a lower-density format than that of the source disk is like trying to pour two quarts of water into a one-quart bottle. Julio's PC isn't quite prepared for such an encounter—and tells him so!

WHAT TO DO: Julio can press **N** (to not continue), put a high-density disk into the target drive (B:), and retype the DISKCOPY command. If the diskette in drive B: is a high-density diskette that has been formatted as a 360K diskette, Julio can press **Y**—which allows DOS to reformat the diskette while copying.

The disk is full

DESCRIPTION: You're in the DOS Shell and have designated a COPY or MOVE command. There isn't enough disk space available to copy your file listed in the dialog box.

EXAMPLE: You're copying several files in the DOS Shell and get this message. The option menu appears, giving you a choice of skipping the file that triggered the message and continuing, or canceling.

Since you know that the file that triggered the message is a large one, you choose to skip this file and continue—causing DOS to ignore copying the current file, and to try copying the next file. This works (this time), because the next file is small enough to fit on your disk.

WHAT TO DO: You can always cancel the operation and try again with a new disk. Or you can fool the Shell into continuing—you can insert a new disk into the drive and select **Skip**. (Just be certain to copy the file you skipped onto the second disk, once this operation ends.)

t

The file doesn't exist

DESCRIPTION: If you try to issue a DOSSHELL command for a file that has been deleted by a previous DOSSHELL operation, you'll get this message.

EXAMPLE: Helen isn't having a good day. She tries to bring up a file that's listed on her screen, but she gets this message. How can this be?

WHAT TO DO: If the DOS Shell screen isn't updated (or refreshed), it will still display a file name, even though the file has been deleted. This is why Helen gets this message. Helen can press **F5** to update the Shell's display, and the file's name will disappear from the directory.

The file is in use by someone else

DESCRIPTION: This DOSSHELL message appears when you're using DOS on a network and try to access a file that someone else is also using. It can also pop up if SHARE.EXE—a file that lets people share files (or stops them from sharing files!)—is not loaded in a multitasking environment (where more than one program is running at a time) on a stand-alone PC.

EXAMPLE: Tom must make changes to his company's employee file. Tom is on a networked system, and so he's not terribly surprised when he tries to access the file and gets this message.

WHAT TO DO: Wait a few moments, and then try again. Or, if you're not on a network, try including SHARE.EXE in your AUTOEXEC.BAT file.

The last file was not restored

DESCRIPTION: You're trying to restore files on a disk, and you get this message.

EXAMPLE: As Lou is restoring files to his hard drive, he gets this Last file not restored message. He checks his hard drive and finds he simply doesn't have enough space to restore all the files. So he deletes some unwanted files and tries again.

WHAT TO DO: Use another diskette to continue backing up files. Put a new disk in the drive and give the RESTORE command again for the files that weren't restored. If your backup files were damaged, those files are lost forever and ever.

t

There is not enough disk space for system files

See *No room for system on destination disk.*

This partition is format protected
You must use DSKSETUP to remove the protection before it can be formatted

See *WARNING: ALL DATA ON NON-REMOVABLE DISK DRIVE X: WILL BE LOST! Proceed with Format (Y/N)?*

Track 0 bad   diskette unusable

DESCRIPTION: There are bad sectors near the beginning of the disk.

EXAMPLE: Gloria wants to format a disk. She pulls one from a dusty drawer in her desk and touches the exposed part as she pops it into the PC. She tries to FORMAT the diskette—and it bombs.

WHAT TO DO: Bad sectors means there's an area on a floppy or hard disk that won't hold your data reliably. In this case, the bad part is at the beginning of the disk—and FORMAT can't accommodate defective sectors if they're at the beginning. You'll probably have to use another diskette. Quality varies among diskette manufacturers, and often varies according to price.

Too many parameters

DESCRIPTION: You've probably typed more than one command on a line, or started to issue one command, then issued another.

EXAMPLE: Geoffery wants to delete all the document files in his root directory, so he types DEL to begin the command. But then he thinks, "Wait a minute, what document files am I going to be deleting, anyway?" So he then types DIR *.DOC and presses Enter.

138

But Geoffery forgot that he had already begun a command, so what he actually entered was DEL DIR *.DOC. And DOS replies *Too many parameters.*

WHAT TO DO: Retype the command.

t

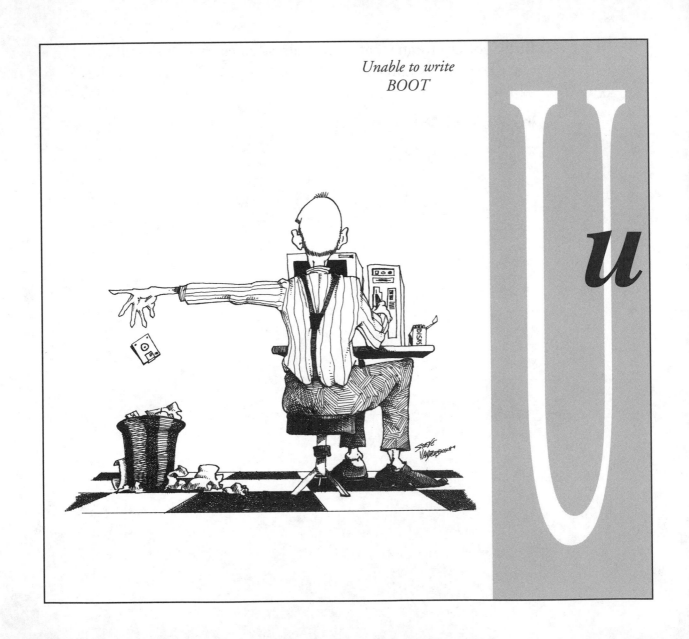

Unable to write
BOOT

Unable to create directory

DESCRIPTION: You're trying to create a directory, and DOS stops you for one of various reasons: you've given a path name that doesn't exist or is too lengthy; the directory you wanted to build has the same name as a file in the current directory; your disk has no free space; the root directory on your current disk is full; or you used illegal characters in your directory name.

EXAMPLE: Maria wants to create a subdirectory to hold all the word processing she does for her boss. She types

```
MD C:\WP\BOSS
```

and gets the Unable to create directory message. Maria wants to see what directories currently exist on her fixed drive, so she types

```
DIR *.
```

which brings up the names of her subdirectories, plus any files without extensions. (Maria doesn't use extensions in her directory names.) Maria discovers that the word processing directory is really named WORD, instead of WP, and so she reissues her command by typing

```
MD C:\WORD\BOSS
```

WHAT TO DO: If this message appears, see if you've entered a true directory and path name. You can also check for a full disk or full root directory, and check to see that no files in the current directory have that same name. Also check for illegal characters in the directory name, such as &, ^, or %.

Unable to read sector
Press A to abort or R to retry

DESCRIPTION: You're trying to bring back some files you accidentally deleted, but it isn't working because the disk or drive you named is holding an unformatted or damaged disk.

This message is unique to the UNDELETE command, which is only available in DOS versions 5.0 and higher.

EXAMPLE: Josie wants to bring back a file she's accidentally deleted from her diskette. She places the diskette that she thinks contains the deleted file into her A: drive and types UNDELETE A*.*. But she has inadvertently picked up the wrong disk; this one is unformatted. So she gets this message.

WHAT TO DO: You can try **R** for Retry. If this doesn't work (and it may not), press **A** to return to the command prompt. This is a good time to be sure you've inserted the correct diskette into the drive named when you first gave the UNDELETE command. There's a very good chance the disk you're using just isn't formatted.

Unable to write BOOT

DESCRIPTION: Whoops! The disk you're trying to format has a defective *Track 0*. (This is the area on the disk where DOS always stores the disk's boot, or startup record, and root directory.)

EXAMPLE: Phil thinks it's a good idea to format a box of diskettes so he has them handy when needed. Everything goes fine, until Phil gets this message on the third diskette out of the box. He saves the diskette and returns it for a refund.

WHAT TO DO: Toss it or return it! Then format another diskette.

Unrecognized command in CONFIG.SYS
Error in CONFIG.SYS line *x*

DESCRIPTION: There's an invalid command line in your CONFIG.SYS file. If you're using DOS 3.x, you won't see the second line of this message.

EXAMPLE: Jack is learning to edit files. He goes into his cousin's file to alter the FILES= statement, but makes a mistake, spelling FILES as FLEES. When Jack reboots the system, this message comes up, listing the line where the misspelled word resides.

WHAT TO DO: It's not a bad idea to watch your screen at boot. Then, if you see an error such as this, you can press **Ctrl-S** (or use the **Pause** key, if you have it) to pause and reflect on the error. Note the message so that you can edit the file.

Unrecognized disk error

DESCRIPTION: This problem arises when disks and drives aren't compatible. You may have told DOS to look in a particular drive for one particular file, but DOS couldn't read the disk and gave you this message instead.

EXAMPLE: Pete is working with a spreadsheet and wants to use the spreadsheet's DOS shell feature. This shell feature lets him temporarily jump to the DOS prompt to see what files are on a diskette he's inserted in the A: drive. Pete gets this message when he tries to bring up the A: directory (DIR A:).

WHAT TO DO: This happens most often if you're using a high-density disk in a low-density drive. It's also possible that the disk has bad sectors. See if your diskette is in a compatible drive. Make sure the diskette is inserted properly and that the drive door is closed. If you still don't get results, you may need to use CHKDSK to see if the disk has bad sectors.

u

Unrecoverable error in directory
Convert directory to file (Y/N)?

DESCRIPTION: Things don't look good. Your PC may have a damaged directory, and you may have lost a lot of good stuff.

EXAMPLE: Seta was running CHKDSK when this message surfaced. DOS looked her squarely in the eye and said that her directory entry—and quite possibly her entire File Allocation Table (FAT)—were messed up really bad (*corrupted*, in fact) by a disk operation. Her directory and its files could be lost.

One possible situation that can create this error is if you have a lot of TSRs in memory when you run a poorly written disk defragmenting program. TSRs, or terminate-and-stay-resident programs, are accessories designed to stay in your PC's random-access memory (RAM) at all times, so that you can activate them with a keystroke—even if another program also is in memory. They can cause problems if they're running at the same time some disk maintenance programs are being run.

WHAT TO DO: Seta's directory entry probably is damaged, and she probably won't be able to bring up files within that directory. Since she keeps current system backups, she can answer **N** to the prompt, remove the directory, and then restore it from her backup.

If she hadn't kept backups, she could have tried to fix the damage herself with a utility program such as Norton's Disk Editor. (Seta is quite a computer whiz.) A beginner would need help—perhaps someone from the local PC club, a university, or computer store.

WARNING ALL DATA ON NON-REMOVABLE DISK DRIVE X: WILL BE LOST!
Proceed with format (Y/N)?

DESCRIPTION: DOS honestly believes that you've said to FORMAT a hard drive. Did you? Or was this an accident? Perhaps a bad dream? (The DOS 3.x version of this message is `This partition is format protected`.) It warns you that if you don't stop, you're going to destroy all the data on your hard disk.

EXAMPLE: Robert prepares to format a disk in drive A:. He types

```
FORMAT C:
```

and gets this warning. He reaches to press N for No, but his finger has a will of its own. . . It's headed for the Y key! Oh no! A moment later, Robert sits up in bed and screams—and then he falls back into a deep sleep. The next day, Robert walks around the office with a slightly anxious feeling; he doesn't know why.

WHAT TO DO: *Very carefully,* put your finger on the **N** to cancel this operation. (If you *really want* this format to happen, press **Y**.) If you format the fixed drive, you can restore it to its original state by giving the name of your hard drive in an UNFORMAT command (available only in DOS 5.0 and above). Never give up—well, at least not too quickly. If you format a fixed drive accidentally, ask a PC user group about what possible software you can use for recovery. There are even private services that help people recover from such dastardly circumstances.

Write error on destination drive

See *Target diskette bad or incompatible*.

Write failure, diskette unusable

DESCRIPTION:　It's just one of those crazy things. You're using the SYS command to transform a diskette into a boot disk—and your PC gives you this terse message.

EXAMPLE:　Ben works in an office. His PC is on the same electrical line as a big copy machine. Sometimes when the copier kicks on and Ben is at his computer, things get messy.

One day, Ben is right in the middle of using SYS to make a boot disk, when the copier starts operating while SYS is writing data to the disk. So the system files aren't transferred.

WHAT TO DO:　The disk is no good. A critical DOS error occurred during the process, and the hidden system files weren't transferred. Throw the disk away, and try making another bootable diskette from scratch.

Write fault error writing device PRN

DESCRIPTION: In DOS 5.0 and above, you'll see this message when you try to print something but have forgotten to turn the printer on.

The equivalent message for other DOS versions would be Not ready writing device PRN for DOS 4.x or Not ready error writing device PRN for DOS 3.x.

EXAMPLE: Sherry is trying to print a copy of her AUTOEXEC.BAT file, so she types

```
COPY AUTOEXEC.BAT>PRN
```

and presses Enter. Since she hasn't turned on the printer's power for the day, DOS reports this error message.

WHAT TO DO: Turn the printer's power on.

W

Write fault error writing drive *x*
Abort, Retry, Fail?

DESCRIPTION: DOS can't write data to the specified disk.

EXAMPLE: PCs are new to Stan. It's kind of scary working with expensive office equipment, especially when you have to figure out everything for yourself! Stan wants to save a backup file of his work, so he puts a diskette in drive B: and instructs his word processor to resave a file on B:. A funny grinding sound comes from the drive, and Stan is really afraid that he's broken the PC.

Then a message that says something about a write error in drive B: comes up on the screen of the word processor.

WHAT TO DO: People who are new to using personal computers often say they feel as though they might break the equipment. If anything goes wrong, their hearts jump into their throats!

There's a good chance here that the disk just isn't properly inserted into the drive. (Maybe it's in upside down!) Stan can check this out, reinsert the disk, and then press **R** to Retry. If he still gets this message, the disk might be bad. He should press **A** to cancel the activity. He'll probably need to toss the diskette and try a new one.

W

Write protect error writing drive *x*
Abort, Retry, Fail?

DESCRIPTION: You've tried to save your work on a write-protected disk.

EXAMPLE: Paula wants to protect her diskette so that no one will destroy her data. She uses 3 1/2-inch diskettes, so she sets the switch manually by sliding the small tile to an open position. If anyone tries to write to her diskette, he or she will get this message.

WHAT TO DO: If the disk has a write-protect tab on it (5 1/4-inch diskettes), or the write-protect switch is set (3 1/2-inch diskettes), you must remove the protection before you can write to the diskette. Be sure, however, to ask yourself *why* the diskette was protected in the first place.

W